KATE HALE

Digital Minimalism

Decluttering Your Digital Life for Mental Clarity

First edition

This book was professionally typeset on Reedsy.
Find out more at reedsy.com

Contents

INTRODUCTION

In the quiet hours of the early morning, Sarah reaches for her smartphone before her eyes are fully open. The soft glow of the screen illuminates her face as she scrolls through a barrage of notifications, emails, and social media updates. By the time she gets out of bed, she's already responded to three work messages, liked a dozen posts, and felt a twinge of anxiety about the day ahead. Sarah's morning routine is not unique – it's a scene playing out in millions of homes across America and around the world.

Welcome to the digital age, where our lives are intricately woven with technology. We carry powerful computers in our pockets, have access to an unfathomable amount of information at our fingertips, and can connect with anyone, anywhere, at any time. The digital revolution has transformed how we work, communicate, learn, and entertain ourselves. It has brought unprecedented convenience, opportunities, and advancements to our lives.

Yet, as we stand midst this digital abundance, a growing disquiet is emerging. Many of us feel overwhelmed, distracted, and somehow less fulfilled despite being more connected than ever before. We find ourselves caught in a paradox: the very tools designed to make our lives easier and more efficient are often the source of stress, anxiety, and a nagging feeling that we're not living life to its fullest potential.

This book, "Digital Minimalism: Decluttering Your Digital Life for Mental Clarity," is born out of this paradox. It's a response to the urgent need for a new approach to our relationship with technology – one that allows us to harness its benefits while mitigating its drawbacks. Digital minimalism is not about rejecting technology outright, but about being intentional and mindful in our use of it. It's about reclaiming our time, attention, and ultimately, our lives from the digital clutter that threatens to overwhelm us.

The Digital Deluge

To understand the need for digital minimalism, we must first comprehend the scale of our digital immersion. According to a 2021 report by e Marketer, the average American adult spends 7 hours and 50 minutes per day interacting with digital media. That's nearly half of our waking hours devoted to screens, apps, and digital platforms. This figure has been steadily increasing year over year, with the COVID-19 pandemic accelerating our digital dependence even further.

But it's not just the quantity of time that's concerning; it's the quality of our digital interactions. We've become a society of multitasks, constantly switching between apps, responding to notifications, and jumping from one piece of content to another. A study by Gloria Mark, a professor of informatics at the University of California, Irvine, found that office workers are interrupted or switch tasks every three minutes and five seconds on average. The same study revealed that it can take up to 23 minutes to fully regain focus after an interruption.

This fragmented attention comes at a cost. Psychologists and neuroscientists are increasingly concerned about the impact of constant digital stimulation on our cognitive functions. Dr. Adam Gazzaley, a neuroscientist at the University of California, San Francisco, warns that our brains are not designed for the kind of rapid task-switching that our digital lives demand. This can lead to decreased productivity, increased stress, and a diminished ability to engage in deep, focused work.

Moreover, our digital habits are reshaping our social interactions and relationships. Sherry Turkle, a professor at MIT and author of "Alone Together," argues that while we're more connected than ever in a superficial sense, many of us are experiencing a profound sense of loneliness and disconnection. We're often physically present but mentally elsewhere, our attention divided between the people around us and the digital world at our fingertips.

The Attention Economy

To fully grasp the need for digital minimalism, we must understand the forces at play in what's known as the "attention economy." In this economy, our attention is the most valuable commodity. Tech companies, advertisers, and content creators are engaged in a fierce competition for our time and focus.

The business models of many tech giants are built on capturing and monetizing our attention. Social media platforms, streaming services, and mobile apps employ sophisticated algorithms and psychological tactics to keep us engaged for as long as possible. Features like infinite scroll, autoplay, and push notifications are not accidents – they're carefully designed to trigger our brain's reward systems and keep us coming back for more.

Tristan Harris, a former Google design ethicist and co-founder of the Center for Humane Technology, has been vocal about the manipulative nature of many digital products. He argues that many apps and platforms are designed to exploit our psychological vulnerabilities, creating what he calls a "race to the bottom of the brain stem." This design philosophy prioritizes engagement metrics over user well-being, often at the expense of our mental health and personal goals.

The result is a digital environment that's increasingly addictive and difficult to navigate mindfully. We find ourselves checking our phones hundreds of times a day, often without conscious intention. A 2019 study by Asurion found that Americans check their phones an average of 96 times a day – that's once every 10 minutes of our waking lives.

The Toll on Our Mental Health

The omnipresence of digital technology in our lives is taking a toll on our mental health. Numerous studies have linked excessive digital media use to increased rates of anxiety, depression, and feelings of loneliness. A 2017 study published in the Clinical Psychological Science journal found a strong correlation between increased screen time and higher rates of depressive symptoms and suicide-related outcomes among adolescents.

Social media, in particular, has been the subject of intense scrutiny. While these platforms can facilitate connection and community, they can also foster comparison, envy, and a distorted view of reality. The carefully curated highlight reels we see of others' lives can leave us feeling inadequate and dissatisfied with our own experiences.

Furthermore, the constant connectivity enabled by our devices has blurred the lines between work and personal life. Many of us feel pressured to be available around the clock, leading to increased stress and burnout. The "always-on" culture has made it difficult to truly disconnect and recharge, impacting our sleep, relationships, and overall well-being.

The Erosion of Deep Work and Creativity

Another casualty of our fragmented digital lives is our capacity for deep work and creative thinking. Cal Newport, author of "Deep Work: Rules for Focused Success in a Distracted World," argues that the ability to focus without distraction on a cognitively demanding task is becoming increasingly rare and increasingly valuable in our economy.

Yet, our digital habits are at odds with this kind of deep, focused work. The constant interruptions and the temptation to quickly check our email or social media make it challenging to enter and maintain a state of flow – that optimal state of consciousness where we're fully immersed in a task and performing at our best.

Moreover, our reliance on digital tools for information and problem-solving may be impacting our creativity. When faced with a challenge, we often turn to Google for quick answers rather than engaging in the kind of deep, reflective thinking that leads to innovative solutions and original ideas. Psychologists warn that this "cognitive offloading" could be weakening our ability to think critically and creatively.

The Environmental and Ethical Considerations

The need for digital minimalism extends beyond personal well-being. Our digital consumption habits have significant environmental and ethical implications that are often overlooked.

The digital economy has a substantial carbon footprint. Data centers, which power our cloud services and internet infrastructure, consume vast amounts of energy. A 2020 study by the International Energy Agency found that data centers account for about 1% of global electricity demand. As our data consumption grows, so does the environmental impact of our digital lives.

There are also ethical considerations surrounding the hardware that powers our digital world. The manufacturing of smartphones, laptops, and other devices often involves the extraction of rare earth minerals, sometimes under questionable labor conditions. Additionally, the rapid pace of technological advancement leads to frequent device upgrades, contributing to the growing problem of electronic waste.

By adopting a more minimalist approach to our digital lives, we can reduce our environmental impact and make more ethical choices about our technology consumption.

The Promise of Digital Minimalism

Given these challenges, the need for a new approach to our digital lives is clear. This is where digital minimalism comes in. Digital minimalism is not about wholesale rejection of technology, but about cultivating a more intentional and balanced relationship with our digital tools.

Digital minimalism offers a path to reclaiming our time, attention, and autonomy in the digital age. It's about using technology in a way that supports our values and goals, rather than letting it dictate our behaviors and thought patterns. By decluttering our digital lives, we can create space for what truly matters – deep work, meaningful relationships, personal growth, and the kind of rich, offline experiences that contribute to a fulfilling life.

The principles of digital minimalism can help us:

1. Regain control over our time and attention
2. Improve our focus and productivity
3. Enhance our mental health and well-being
4. Foster deeper, more meaningful relationships
5. Rediscover the joy of offline activities and experiences
6. Make more conscious and ethical technology choices

Throughout this book, we'll explore practical strategies for implementing digital minimalism in various aspects of our lives. We'll learn how to declutter our devices, manage our digital communications, cultivate healthier social media habits, and create sustainable digital routines that align with our personal values and goals.

A Call to Action

As we embark on this journey towards digital minimalism, it's important to recognize that change won't happen overnight. Our digital habits are deeply ingrained, and the forces of the attention economy are powerful. But with awareness, intention, and consistent effort, we can transform our relationship with technology.

This book is not about demonizing technology or advocating for a luddite existence. Rather, it's an invitation to step back, reassess our digital lives, and make conscious choices about how we engage with the digital world. It's about creating a lifestyle where technology serves us, not the other way around.

In the chapters that follow, we'll delve deeper into the principles of digital minimalism and explore practical strategies for decluttering our digital lives. We'll hear from experts in psychology, neuroscience, and technology ethics, and we'll learn from real-life examples of people who have successfully embraced digital minimalism.

Whether you're feeling overwhelmed by digital clutter, concerned about your technology habits, or simply curious about how to live more intentionally in the digital age, this book offers a road map to a more balanced and fulfilling relationship with technology.

As we close this introduction, I invite you to reflect on your own digital life. How much of your time and attention is consumed by digital media? How often do you find yourself mindlessly reaching for your phone or scrolling through social media? How has your relationship with technology impacted your work, your relationships, and your sense of well-being?

The journey to digital minimalism starts with these questions. It starts with a willingness to examine our habits, challenge our assumptions, and make intentional choices about our digital consumption. It's not always an easy path, but it's one that leads to greater clarity, focus, and fulfillment in our increasingly digital world.

So, let's begin this journey together. Let's explore how we can harness the incredible power of technology while reclaiming our time, attention, and lives from digital clutter. Welcome to the world of digital minimalism – your path to a clearer, more intentional digital life starts here.

The Evolution of Digital Overload

T o truly grasp the concept of digital minimalism and its importance in our lives, we must first understand how we arrived at our current state of digital overload. This chapter will explore the evolution of digital technology, from the early days of personal computing to the omnipresent, always-on devices we carry with us today. We'll examine how this technological progression has fundamentally altered our relationship with information, communication, and even our own attention.

From Desktop to Pocket: The Rise of Always-On Technology

The Desktop Era

Our journey begins in the late 20th century with the advent of personal computers. In the 1980s and early 1990s, computers were primarily stationary devices, confined to desks in homes and offices. These machines, while revolutionary, had limited connectivity. The internet was in its infancy, and most people's digital experiences were isolated and intermittent.

The typical computer user of this era would sit down at their desk, boot up their machine (a process that could take several minutes), and engage in specific, intentional tasks. When work was done, or when it was time to leave the house, the computer was shut down, and digital engagement ceased. This natural boundary between digital and physical worlds helped maintain a clear delineation between work and personal life, between online and offline existence.

The Internet Revolution

The late 1990s and early 2000s saw the rapid growth of the internet and email. Suddenly, our computers became portals to a vast world of information and communication. This shift brought immense benefits - instant access to knowledge, the ability to connect with people across the globe, and new forms of entertainment and commerce.

However, it also marked the beginning of what we now recognize as digital overload. Email, in particular, became a source of constant input, blurring the lines between work and personal time. The need to "check email" became a frequent compulsion, marking one of the first steps towards our always-on digital culture.

The Mobile Revolution

The true paradigm shift came with the widespread adoption of smartphones, epitomized by the launch of the iPhone in 2007. Suddenly, the power of a computer and the connectivity of the internet were available in our pockets, accessible at all times.

This shift from desktop to pocket computing cannot be overstated in its impact on our digital lives. No longer were we tethered to a desk to access the digital world. Now, that world was with us constantly, accessible with a tap or a swipe. The smartphone became our alarm clock, our map, our camera, our entertainment center, and our primary means of communication.

The ability to be constantly connected brought undeniable benefits. We could navigate unfamiliar cities with ease, stay in touch with loved ones across vast distances, and access information on any topic at a moment's notice. But it also meant that the boundaries between our digital and physical lives began to dissolve.

The App Economy

With smartphones came app stores, offering a seemingly endless array of applications for every conceivable purpose. This explosion of apps further integrated digital technology into every aspect of our lives. We now had apps for tracking our fitness, managing our finances, controlling our home devices, and even monitoring our sleep.

While each app might solve a specific problem or offer a particular benefit, the cumulative effect was a deepening of our dependence on digital technology. Each new app demanded a slice of our attention, contributing to the growing sense of digital overload.

The Internet of Things

The most recent phase in this evolution is the rise of the Internet of Things (IoT). Now, it's not just our phones and computers that are connected, but our thermostats, refrigerators, cars, and even our light bulbs. This expansion of connectivity into the physical world around us has further blurred the lines between online and offline life.

The promise of IoT is a more efficient, convenient world where our devices anticipate and meet our needs. However, it also means that we're never truly disconnected. Our digital lives now extend into every corner of our physical spaces, creating an always-on, always-connected existence that would have been unimaginable just a few decades ago.

The Attention Economy: How Tech Companies Compete for Your Time

As our devices became more powerful and our connectivity more constant, a new economic model emerged: the attention economy. In this paradigm, human attention is treated as a scarce commodity and a form of currency. Tech companies, advertisers, and content creators compete fiercely for our attention, employing increasingly sophisticated tactics to capture and retain it.

The Business Model of Attention

Many of the world's most valuable companies - including Facebook (now Meta), Google, and Twitter - have built their business models around capturing and monetizing human attention. These companies offer their core services for free, generating revenue instead through advertising. The more time users spend on their platforms, the more ads they can show, and the more data they can collect to refine their targeting.

This business model creates a strong incentive for these companies to make their products as engaging - or, some would argue, addictive - as possible. Features like infinite scroll, autoplay videos, and push notifications are not accidental; they're carefully designed to keep us engaged for as long as possible.

The Science of Persuasive Technology

To compete in the attention economy, tech companies employ teams of psychologists, neuroscientists, and behavioral economists to design their products. These experts draw on a deep understanding of human psychology to create features that exploit our cognitive biases and trigger our brain's reward systems.

For example, the "pull-to-refresh" mechanism used in many social media apps mimics the variable reward system of slot machines, a technique known to be highly addictive. Similarly, the red notification badges we see on our app icons trigger a sense of urgency and a fear of missing out (FOMO), compelling us to check our devices repeatedly.

The Cost of "Free"

While many of these attention-capturing services are ostensibly free to use, we pay for them with our time, our attention, and our personal data. This arrangement has led to what Tristan Harris, a former Google design ethicist, calls a "race to the bottom of the brain stem" - a competition to see who can most effectively grab and hold our attention, regardless of the content's quality or its impact on our well-being.

The Fragmentation of Attention

One of the most significant consequences of the attention economy is the fragmentation of our attention. With multiple apps and platforms constantly vying for our focus, we find ourselves switching tasks more frequently, multitasking more often, and struggling to engage in deep, focused work.

A study by Gloria Mark at the University of California, Irvine, found that office workers are interrupted or switch tasks every three minutes on average. After each interruption, it can take up to 23 minutes to return to the original task fully. In an eight-hour workday, that translates to a significant loss of productivity and an increase in stress.

The Psychological Impact of Information Overload

As we've transitioned into this always-on, information-rich digital environment, our brains have struggled to keep pace. The sheer volume of information we encounter daily, combined with the constant demands on our attention, is taking a toll on our cognitive functions and our mental health.

Cognitive Overload

Our brains have limited capacity for processing information. When we exceed this capacity - a state known as cognitive overload - our ability to think clearly, make decisions, and retain information is impaired.

In the digital age, we're constantly bombarding our brains with information. Every email, every social media post, every push notification demands cognitive resources. When this input exceeds our brain's processing capacity, we experience symptoms such as difficulty concentrating, increased error rates, and a general sense of mental fatigue.

Dr. Daniel Levitin, a neuroscientist and author of "The Organized Mind," explains that information overload can trigger the release of cortisol, the stress hormone. This not only makes us feel anxious and overwhelmed but can also cloud our judgment and impair our decision-making abilities.

Decision Fatigue

Related to cognitive overload is the phenomenon of decision fatigue. Our digital lives require us to make countless small decisions throughout the day: which emails to respond to, which social media posts to engage with, which notifications to act on. Each decision, no matter how small, depletes our mental energy.

As we make more and more decisions, the quality of our decision-making tends to deteriorate. We may become more impulsive, more likely to take shortcuts, or simply choose to avoid making decisions altogether. This can lead to poor choices in both our digital lives and our physical world.

Attention Deficit Trait

Psychiatrist Edward Hallowell has identified a phenomenon he calls Attention Deficit Trait (ADT), which he describes as "a condition induced by modern life, in which you've become so busy attending to so many inputs and outputs that you become increasingly distracted, irritable, impulsive, restless and, over the long term, underachieving."

Unlike Attention Deficit Disorder (ADD), which has a neurological basis, ADT is an environmentally induced response to the overwhelming demands on our attention in the digital age. Hallowell argues that many of us are experiencing symptoms similar to ADD as a result of our constant digital engagement.

The Illusion of Productivity

Our digital tools promise to make us more productive, and in many ways, they do. We can communicate instantly, access information rapidly, and perform complex tasks with the help of sophisticated software. However, the constant stream of digital inputs can also create an illusion of productivity that masks a deeper inefficiency.

We may feel busy and engaged as we respond to emails, check social media, and juggle multiple digital tasks. But this busyness often comes at the expense of deep, focused work that truly moves our most important projects forward. Cal Newport, in his book "Deep Work," argues that the ability to focus without distraction on a cognitively demanding task is becoming increasingly rare and increasingly valuable in our economy.

Impact on Memory and Learning

Our reliance on digital devices is also changing how we remember and learn. The ready availability of information at our fingertips means we're less likely to commit facts to memory. Instead, we're developing what some researchers call "transactive memory" - we remember where to find information rather than remembering the information itself.

While this can be an efficient way of managing the vast amount of information available to us, it may also be changing how we think and solve problems. There's a concern that we're losing the ability to make creative connections between disparate pieces of information - connections that often lead to innovation and insight.

Social Media and Mental Health

The rise of social media has brought its own set of psychological challenges. While these platforms can facilitate connection and community, they can also foster comparison, envy, and a distorted view of reality.

Numerous studies have linked heavy social media use to increased rates of anxiety, depression, and loneliness. The carefully curated highlight reels we see of others' lives can leave us feeling inadequate and dissatisfied with our own experiences. The constant quest for likes and shares can create a cycle of seeking external validation that can be detrimental to our self-esteem and mental well-being.

Digital Addiction

For some individuals, the psychological impact of our digital world manifests as a form of addiction. Internet Gaming Disorder is now recognized in the Diagnostic and Statistical Manual of Mental Disorders (DSM-5), and there's ongoing debate about whether broader forms of internet or smartphone addiction should be officially recognized.

Whether or not it meets the clinical definition of addiction, many people report feeling a compulsive need to check their devices, experiencing anxiety when separated from their phones, and struggling to control their digital habits. This loss of control over our digital engagement can have serious implications for our mental health, our relationships, and our overall quality of life.

The Challenge of Disconnecting

Perhaps one of the most insidious psychological impacts of our always-on digital world is the difficulty we face in truly disconnecting. The fear of missing out (FOMO) can make us feel anxious about being away from our devices. The blurring of work and personal life makes it challenging to establish clear boundaries for digital engagement.

Even when we do manage to step away from our devices, many of us find it difficult to be present in the moment. Our minds have become so accustomed to constant stimulation that we may feel bored or restless without digital input. This difficulty in disconnecting not only impacts our ability to relax and recharge but can also affect our relationships and our ability to engage deeply with the world around us.

In conclusion, the evolution from desktop computing to always-on mobile technology has dramatically transformed our relationship with the digital world. While bringing unprecedented access to information and connectivity, it has also led to an attention economy that often prioritizes engagement over well-being. The resulting information overload has significant psychological impacts, affecting everything from our cognitive functions to our mental health.

Understanding this evolution and its impacts is the first step in reclaiming control over our digital lives. By recognizing how we arrived at this state of digital overload, we can begin to make more intentional choices about our technology use. In the following chapters, we'll explore strategies for mitigating these negative impacts and cultivating a healthier, more balanced relationship with digital technology.

Assessing Your Digital Landscape

I n our journey towards digital minimalism, the first crucial step is to gain a clear understanding of our current digital habits and environment. This chapter will guide you through the process of conducting a personal digital audit, help you identify the major time sinks and attention drains in your digital life, and assist you in recognizing the habits and triggers that drive your digital behavior.

Conducting a Personal Digital Audit

A personal digital audit is a comprehensive review of your digital life. It involves taking stock of all your digital assets, activities, and habits. This process can be eye-opening, sometimes even uncomfortable, but it's essential for making informed decisions about your digital consumption.

Step 1: Inventory Your Digital Devices

Begin by listing all the digital devices you own and use regularly. This might include:

- Smartphones
    - Tablets
    - Laptops
    - Desktop computers
    - Smart watches

- E-readers
- Smart home devices (smart speakers, smart TVs, etc.)

For each device, note how often you use it and for what purposes. This will give you an initial overview of your digital touch points.

Step 2: Catalog Your Digital Accounts

Next, make a list of all your digital accounts. This includes:

- Email accounts
  - Social media profiles
  - Streaming services
  - Online shopping accounts
  - Cloud storage services
  - Digital subscriptions
  - Gaming platforms
  - Messaging apps

As you compile this list, you may be surprised by the number of digital services you're subscribed to. For each account, note the last time you used it and whether it still provides value to you.

Step 3: Track Your Screen Time

Most smartphones now have built-in screen time tracking features. For a week, use these tools to monitor how much time you spend on your devices and which apps you use most frequently. If you use computers frequently, consider using time-tracking software like Rescue Time or Manic Time to get a complete picture of your digital time expenditure.

Keep a log of your findings, noting:

- Total daily screen time
  - Most used apps and websites
  - Times of day when your usage peaks

Step 4: Assess Your Digital Communication

Examine your digital communication habits:

- How many emails do you receive and send daily?
  - How often do you check your inbox?
  - Which messaging apps do you use most frequently?
  - How much time do you spend on voice or video calls?

Step 5: Evaluate Your Digital Content Consumption

Consider your digital content consumption habits:

- How much time do you spend on social media daily?
  - How many hours of video content (TV shows, movies, YouTube videos) do you watch?
  - How much time do you spend reading digital content (e-books, articles, blogs)?
  - How often do you play digital games?

Step 6: Reflect on Your Findings

After collecting all this data, take some time to reflect on your findings. Ask yourself:

- Are you surprised by any of the results?
  - Which digital activities seem to be taking up more time than you realized?
  - Are there any digital habits you'd like to change?
  - How do you feel about your current level of digital engagement?

This reflection will set the stage for the next phases of your digital minimalism journey.

Identifying Time Sinks and Attention Drains

Now that you have a clear picture of your digital landscape, it's time to identify the elements that are consuming disproportionate amounts of your time and attention. These are your digital time sinks and attention drains.

Recognizing Time Sinks

Time sinks are activities that consume a lot of time but provide little value in return. In the digital realm, common time sinks include:

1. Endless Scrolling: Social media platforms are designed to keep you engaged for as long as possible. The infinite scroll feature can lead to spending far more time than intended on these apps.

2. Binge-Watching: Streaming services that automatically play the next episode can turn a quick TV break into hours of watching.

3. Notification Checking: The habit of frequently checking notifications, even when no alert has sounded, can accumulate into significant lost time over a day.

4. Email Over management: Constantly checking and responding to emails, especially those that aren't urgent, can be a major time sink.

5. Mindless Web Surfing: Aimlessly clicking from one website to another without a specific purpose can eat up large chunks of time.

To identify your personal time sinks:

- Review your screen time data and look for apps or activities where you spend a lot of time but gain little benefit.
   - Keep a time log for a few days, noting how you spend your digital time and how you feel afterward.
   - Reflect on moments when you've looked up from your device and wondered where the time went.

Identifying Attention Drains

Attention drains are digital elements that frequently interrupt your focus or demand your attention, even if they don't necessarily consume large amounts of time. These can include:

1. Push Notifications: Alerts from various apps that interrupt your current activity and pull your attention elsewhere.

2. Email Alerts: New email notifications that break your concentration, even if you don't immediately respond.

3. Group Chats: Active group conversations that constantly ping for your attention.

4. Breaking News Alerts: News app notifications that create a sense of urgency to stay updated.

5. App Update Notifications: Frequent reminders to update your apps or operating system.

To identify your attention drains:

- Notice what digital elements most often interrupt you when you're trying to focus.
   - Review your notification settings and consider which ones you find

genuinely useful versus disruptive.

- Reflect on moments when you've felt scattered or unable to concentrate, and identify if digital interruptions played a role.

The Intersection of Time and Attention

Some digital activities can be both time sinks and attention drains. Social media, for instance, can consume large amounts of time through endless scrolling (time sink) while also frequently interrupting you with notifications (attention drain).

Identifying these dual offenders is particularly important as they have an outsizes impact on your digital well-being.

Quantifying the Impact

To truly understand the impact of these time sinks and attention drains, try to quantify their effects:

- Estimate how much time you spend daily on identified time sinks.
- Count how many times per day your attention is pulled away by digital interruptions.
- Consider the opportunity cost: what could you be doing with that time and uninterrupted attention?

This quantification will help you prioritize which areas to address first in your journey towards digital minimalism.

Recognizing Digital Habits and Triggers

Our digital behaviors are often driven by habitual patterns and specific triggers. Recognizing these can be a powerful step in regaining control over our digital lives.

Understanding Habits

Habits are automated behaviors that we perform without much conscious thought. In the digital realm, habitual behaviors might include:

- Checking your phone first thing in the morning
    - Opening social media apps during moments of boredom
    - Responding immediately to every notification
    - Watching videos while eating meals
    - Scrolling through news feeds before bed

To identify your digital habits:

1. Keep a Habit Journal: For a week, jot down every time you engage with a digital device. Note what you did, when you did it, and what prompted the action.

2. Look for Patterns: Review your journal and screen time data to identify recurring behaviors.

3. Assess Automatically: Consider which digital behaviors you do almost without thinking.

4. Evaluate Context: Notice in what situations or at what times of day certain digital habits occur most frequently.

Identifying Triggers

Triggers are the cues that prompt us to engage in habitual behaviors. In the context of digital habits, triggers can be external (environmental cues) or internal (emotional states).

Common external triggers include:

- Notification sounds or vibrations
  - Seeing others use their devices
  - Specific locations (like your desk or bed)
  - Certain times of day (like lunch breaks or bedtime)

Internal triggers might include emotional states such as:

- Boredom
  - Loneliness
  - Stress
  - Anxiety
  - Procrastination
  - FOMO (Fear of Missing Out)

To identify your personal triggers:

1. Pause Before Acting: The next time you reach for your device, pause and ask yourself why. What just happened externally or internally to prompt this action?

2. Track Emotional States: When you engage in digital activities, note your emotional state. Are you seeking distraction, connection, or information?

3. Conduct a Trigger Audit: For each of your identified digital habits, try to pinpoint the specific trigger that usually precedes it.

4. Examine Your Environment: Look around your physical spaces. Are there aspects of your environment that encourage digital engagement?

The Habit Loop

Understanding the concept of the "habit loop" can be helpful in recognizing and potentially changing your digital habits. As described by Charles Higgins in "The Power of Habit," the habit loop consists of three elements:

1. Cue (Trigger): The signal that initiates the behavior.
   2. Routine: The behavior itself.
   3. Reward: The benefit you gain from the behavior.

For example:

- Cue: You feel bored (internal trigger).
  - Routine: You open Instagram and start scrolling.
  - Reward: You feel entertained and connected.

By identifying each element of your digital habit loops, you can start to see opportunities for intervention and change.

Assessing the Strength of Habits and Triggers

Not all habits and triggers are created equal. Some have a stronger hold on us than others. To assess the strength of your digital habits and triggers:

1. Attempt Resistance: Try to resist acting on a trigger. How difficult is it? How do you feel?

2. Measure Frequency: How often does the habit occur? More frequent habits are typically more ingrained.

3. Evaluate Emotional Impact: How do you feel if you can't engage in the habitual behavior? Stronger emotional responses often indicate stronger habits.

4. Consider Duration: How long have you had this habit? Longer-standing habits are usually more challenging to change.

Recognizing Positive Digital Habits

While much of this assessment focuses on problematic digital behaviors, it's also important to recognize positive digital habits. These might include:

- Using productivity apps to manage tasks effectively
    - Engaging in online learning
    - Connecting meaningfully with long-distance friends and family
    - Using digital tools for creative expression

Identifying these positive habits can help you focus on what you want to preserve and enhance in your digital life as you move towards minimalism.

Bringing It All Together

As you complete this assessment of your digital landscape, take some time to synthesize your findings. Create a summary that includes:

1. Your key digital devices and accounts
    2. Your primary time sinks and attention drains
    3. Your most significant digital habits and their associated triggers
    4. Any positive digital habits you want to maintain or strengthen

This summary will serve as a road map for the next steps in your digital minimalism journey. It will help you identify where to focus your efforts for maximum impact and guide you in creating a more intentional relationship with technology.

Remember, the goal of this assessment is not to judge or criticize your current digital habits. Rather, it's to bring awareness to your digital behaviors and their impacts on your life. This awareness is the foundation upon which you can build a more mindful and intentional approach to technology use.

In the next chapters, we'll explore strategies for addressing the time sinks, attention drains, and habitual behaviors you've identified. We'll also discuss how to cultivate new, more positive digital habits that align with your values and goals. By starting with this thorough assessment of your digital landscape, you're taking a crucial first step towards a more balanced and fulfilling digital life.

The Cost of Digital Clutter

As we've explored in previous chapters, our lives have become increasingly intertwined with digital technology. While this digital integration has brought numerous benefits, it has also introduced new challenges. In this chapter, we'll examine the hidden costs of digital clutter - the accumulated digital noise that pervades our daily lives. We'll focus on three main areas: productivity and focus, mental health and well-being, and the impact on our relationships and social interactions.

Decreased Productivity and Focus

One of the most significant costs of digital clutter is its impact on our productivity and ability to focus. In an age where information and distractions are just a click away, maintaining concentration and getting things done has become increasingly challenging.

The Myth of Multitasking

Many of us pride ourselves on our ability to multitask, juggling multiple digital streams simultaneously. However, research consistently shows that multitasking is largely a myth. What we're actually doing is task-switching, rapidly moving our attention from one task to another.

Dr. David Meyer, a cognitive scientist at the University of Michigan, has found that switching tasks can cost as much as 40% of someone's productive time. This is because our brains need time to refocus and reorient with each switch. The more complex the tasks, the more time we lose in this switching process.

In the digital realm, we're constantly encouraged to multitask:
- Checking email while working on a report
- Responding to instant messages while on a video call
- Scrolling through social media while watching a movie

Each of these switches comes with a cognitive cost, reducing our overall productivity and the quality of our work.

The Fragmentation of Attention

Digital clutter doesn't just affect us when we're actively engaging with our devices. The mere presence of digital distractions can fragment our attention. A study by Adrian Ward and colleagues at the University of Texas found that the mere presence of one's smartphone, even when turned off and face down, reduced cognitive capacity. Participants who left their phones in another room performed significantly better on tests of cognitive capacity than those who had their phones on the desk or in their pocket or bag.

This fragmentation of attention can lead to:

1. Increased error rates: When our attention is divided, we're more likely to make mistakes.
2. Reduced creativity: Deep, creative thinking requires sustained focus, which is harder to achieve in a digitally cluttered environment.
3. Longer completion times: Tasks take longer when we're constantly interrupted or distracted.
4. Decreased quality of work: Our best work typically requires our full attention and effort.

The Toll on Deep Work

Cal Newport, in his book "Deep Work," argues that the ability to focus without distraction on a cognitively demanding task is becoming increasingly rare and increasingly valuable in our economy. Yet, digital clutter directly opposes this kind of deep, focused work.

Constant notifications, the temptation to quickly check email or social media, and the habit of immediate responsiveness cultivated by digital communication all erode our capacity for deep work. This erosion can have serious implications for our professional development and career progression, especially in fields that require complex problem-solving or creative thinking.

The Pressure of Digital Presenteeism

Digital technology has also given rise to a culture of "digital presenteeism" - the feeling that we need to be always available and responsive. This pressure can lead to:

1. Constant task-switching: Feeling the need to immediately respond to every email or message.
   2. Difficulty in prioritizing: When everything seems urgent, it's hard to focus on what's truly important.
   3. Extended working hours: The ability to work from anywhere can lead to working all the time.
   4. Reduced recovery time: Constant connectivity makes it harder to truly disconnect and recharge.

All of these factors contribute to decreased productivity and focus, making it harder to perform at our best in both our professional and personal lives.

Impact on Mental Health and Well-being

The costs of digital clutter extend beyond productivity, significantly impacting our mental health and overall well-being.

Digital Overwhelm and Stress

The sheer volume of digital information we encounter daily can lead to a state of digital overwhelm. Our brains have limited capacity for processing information, and when we exceed this capacity, we experience cognitive overload. This state can manifest as:

1. Increased stress levels: Constant digital input can trigger our stress response, leading to elevated cortisol levels.

2. Decision fatigue: The multitude of small decisions required in our digital lives can deplete our mental energy.

3. Feelings of inadequacy: Struggling to keep up with the flood of information can lead to feelings of falling behind or not being good enough.

Dr. Daniel Levitin, neuroscientist and author of "The Organized Mind," explains that information overload can cause our brains to become easily fatigued, leading to poor decision-making and increased anxiety.

The Anxiety of Constant Connectivity

Our always-on digital culture has given rise to new forms of anxiety:

1. FOMO (Fear of Missing Out): The fear that if we disconnect, we might miss important information or social opportunities.

2. Nomophobia: The fear of being without a mobile device, or beyond mobile phone contact.

3. Phantom Vibration Syndrome: The false sensation of your phone vibrating, even when it hasn't.

These digital-age anxieties can contribute to a general sense of unease and make it difficult to relax and be present in the moment.

The Impact on Sleep

Digital clutter often extends into our bedrooms, affecting the quantity and quality of our sleep. The blue light emitted by screens can suppress melatonin production, making it harder to fall asleep. Additionally, the stimulating nature of digital content can keep our minds active when we should be winding down.

Poor sleep has wide-ranging effects on our mental health, including:

1. Increased risk of depression and anxiety
   2. Impaired emotional regulation
   3. Reduced cognitive function
   4. Decreased ability to cope with stress

Social Media and Self-Esteem

While social media can facilitate connection, it can also negatively impact our self-esteem and overall mental well-being. Constant exposure to curated highlights of others' lives can lead to:

1. Social comparison: Feeling that our lives don't measure up to what we see online.
   2. Validation-seeking behavior: Becoming overly dependent on likes and comments for self-worth.
   3. FOMO and anxiety: Feeling anxious about missing out on social events or experiences.

A study published in the Journal of Social and Clinical Psychology found a causal link between Facebook use and decreases in well-being, particularly in how people feel moment-to-moment and how satisfied they are with their lives.

Digital Addiction

For some individuals, digital clutter can lead to addictive behaviors. Internet Gaming Disorder is now recognized in the DSM-5, and there's ongoing debate about broader forms of internet or smartphone addiction.

Signs of digital addiction can include:

1. Feeling anxious or irritable when unable to use digital devices
    2. Neglecting other activities to spend time online
    3. Unsuccessful attempts to cut back on digital use
    4. Losing track of time when using digital devices

Whether or not it meets the clinical definition of addiction, problematic digital use can significantly impact mental health and overall quality of life.

The Erosion of Mindfulness

Our digitally cluttered lives often leave little room for mindfulness - the practice of being fully present and engaged in the current moment. Constant digital engagement can lead to:

1. Difficulty in being present in face-to-face interactions
    2. Reduced ability to enjoy simple pleasures
    3. Decreased self-awareness and emotional intelligence

Mindfulness has been shown to have numerous mental health benefits, including reduced stress and anxiety, improved emotional regulation, and increased overall well-being. The erosion of mindfulness due to digital clutter represents a significant cost to our mental health.

Relationships and Social Interactions in the Digital Age

While digital technology has provided new ways to connect, it has also fundamentally altered how we interact with each other, sometimes to the detriment of our relationships.

The Paradox of Connection

In our digitally connected world, we can instantly communicate with people across the globe. Yet, many people report feeling more isolated and lonely than ever. This paradox of connection arises from several factors:

1. Quantity over quality: Digital communication often favors quick, surface-level interactions over deep, meaningful conversations.
2. Reduced face-to-face interaction: The ease of digital communication can lead to fewer in-person interactions, which are crucial for building strong relationships.
3. The illusion of connection: Having hundreds of online friends doesn't necessarily translate to having strong, supportive relationships.

A study published in the American Journal of Preventive Medicine found that heavy social media users were twice as likely to report experiencing social isolation.

The Impact on Intimate Relationships

Digital clutter can significantly affect our most intimate relationships:

1. Phubbing: The act of snubbing someone in favor of your phone. This behavior can lead to decreased relationship satisfaction and increased conflict.
2. Decreased intimacy: Excessive device use can reduce opportunities for intimate conversations and shared experiences.
3. Trust issues: Digital communication can sometimes lead to misunder-

standings or provide opportunities for secretive behavior, potentially eroding trust.

A study by the Pew Research Center found that 51% of adults in romantic relationships have felt their partner was distracted by their cell phone when they were trying to have a conversation.

Changes in Social Skills and Empathy

Over reliance on digital communication may be affecting our ability to interact effectively in person:

1. Reduced nonverbal communication skills: Less practice in reading facial expressions and body language.
   2. Decreased comfort with silence: The constant stimulation of digital environments can make silent moments in conversation feel uncomfortable.
   3. Shortened attention spans: The rapid pace of digital interaction may make it harder to engage in lengthy, in-depth conversations.

Some researchers have raised concerns about the impact of digital technology on empathy, particularly among younger generations who have grown up with smartphones and social media. While the research is still evolving, there's concern that reduced face-to-face interaction could lead to decreased ability to understand and share the feelings of others.

The Pressure of Digital Self-Presentation

Social media and other digital platforms create pressure to curate and present an idealized version of ourselves:

1. Anxiety about self-image: Constant comparison to others' curated lives can lead to anxiety and dissatisfaction with one's own life.
   2. Reduced authenticity: The pressure to present a perfect image can make

it harder to be genuine and vulnerable in relationships.

3. Fear of judgment: Knowing that any moment could be captured and shared online can lead to self-consciousness in social situations.

The Erosion of Boundaries

Digital technology has blurred the boundaries between different aspects of our lives:

1. Work-life balance: The ability to work from anywhere can make it difficult to fully disconnect from work.

2. Public vs. private life: Social media can make private moments public, sometimes with unintended consequences.

3. Social circles: Digital platforms often flatten our social circles, putting close friends, acquaintances, colleagues, and family all on the same level.

This erosion of boundaries can lead to increased stress and difficulty in managing different roles and relationships.

The Impact on Family Dynamics

Digital clutter can significantly affect family relationships:

1. Decreased family time: Individual family members engrossed in their devices may spend less quality time together.

2. Distracted parenting: Parents distracted by devices may be less responsive to their children's needs.

3. Generational divides: Differences in digital habits between generations can lead to misunderstandings and conflicts.

A study published in the journal Child Development found that parents' problematic digital technology use was associated with lower-quality parent-child interactions.

The Challenge of Digital Etiquette

As our lives have become more digital, new social norms and etiquette have had to evolve. However, this evolution is ongoing and often unclear, leading to potential social friction:

1. Response time expectations: Digital communication has created an expectation of immediate response, which can be stressful and unrealistic.
2. Appropriate use of devices in social settings: There's often uncertainty about when it's acceptable to use devices in various social situations.
3. Online communication tone: The lack of nonverbal cues in digital communication can lead to misunderstandings and conflicts.

The Value of Digital Connections

While this section has focused on the costs of digital clutter to our relationships, it's important to acknowledge that digital technology has also provided valuable ways to maintain and even deepen relationships:

1. Long-distance connections: Digital tools allow us to stay connected with loved ones regardless of physical distance.
2. Community building: Online platforms can help people find and connect with like-minded individuals.
3. Support networks: Digital spaces can provide valuable support for people dealing with specific challenges or conditions.

The key is finding a balance that allows us to reap these benefits without letting digital clutter overwhelm our relationships.

In conclusion, the costs of digital clutter are significant and far-reaching, impacting our productivity, mental health, and relationships. By understanding these costs, we can begin to see the value of digital minimalism - not as a rejection of technology, but as a way to use it more intentionally and effectively. In the following chapters, we'll explore strategies for decluttering our digital lives and cultivating a healthier relationship with technology, allowing us to minimize these costs while maximizing the benefits of our digital tools.

Defining Digital Minimalism

I n our increasingly connected world, the concept of digital minimalism has emerged as a response to the overwhelming presence of technology in our lives. But what exactly is digital minimalism? How does it differ from simply using less technology? And how can we implement it in a way that enhances rather than diminishes our lives? In this chapter, we'll explore these questions and lay the groundwork for a more intentional relationship with technology.

Core Philosophies and Values

Digital minimalism is more than just a set of practices; it's a philosophy of technology use. At its core, digital minimalism is about being intentional with our digital lives, focusing on what truly matters, and eliminating digital clutter. Let's explore the key philosophies and values that underpin this approach.

1. Intersectionality

The cornerstone of digital minimalism is intersectionality. This means being deliberate about what digital tools we use, how we use them, and why we use them. It's about moving from passive consumption to active choice.

Cal Newport, who popularized the term "digital minimalism" in his book of the same name, defines it as:

"A philosophy of technology use in which you focus your online time on a small number of carefully selected and optimized activities that strongly support things you value, and then happily miss out on everything else."

This definition highlights the importance of aligning our digital use with our values and goals. It's not about using technology less, but about using it more purposefully.

2. Quality Over Quantity

Digital minimalism emphasizes the quality of our digital interactions over their quantity. It recognizes that not all screen time is created equal. An hour spent in a meaningful video call with a loved one is fundamentally different from an hour of mindless scrolling.

This philosophy encourages us to curate our digital experiences, focusing on those that provide real value and eliminating those that don't. It's about creating a digital life that's rich in quality, even if it's lighter in quantity.

3. Digital Decluttering

Just as physical minimalism involves decluttering our physical spaces, digital minimalism involves decluttering our digital spaces. This means:

- Unsubscribing from email lists that don't provide value
  - Following social media accounts that don't inspire or inform us
  - Deleting apps that we don't use or that don't align with our goals
  - Organizing our digital files and cleaning up our digital workspace

The goal is to create digital environments that support focus and reduce unnecessary distractions.

4. Mindfulness and Presence

Digital minimalism places a high value on mindfulness and being present in the moment. It recognizes that our constant connectivity can often pull us away from the present, whether we're checking our phones during a conversation or thinking about work emails during family time.

By encouraging us to be more intentional with our technology use, digital minimalism helps us be more present in our offline lives. It's about creating space for real-world experiences and face-to-face interactions.

5. Digital Empowerment

Importantly, digital minimalism is not about rejecting technology. Instead, it's about empowering ourselves to use technology in a way that serves us, rather than feeling controlled by it. It's about being the masters of our digital tools, not their servants.

This philosophy recognizes the immense benefits that technology can bring to our lives when used intentionally. The goal is to harness these benefits while minimizing the downsides.

6. Continuous Evaluation

Finally, digital minimalism involves a commitment to continuously evaluating our relationship with technology. As new tools emerge and our lives change, what serves us well today may not serve us well tomorrow.

Digital minimalists regularly reflect on their technology use, asking questions like:
   - Is this tool still adding value to my life?
   - Are there better ways to use this technology?
   - Has this digital habit aligned with my values and goals?

This ongoing evaluation ensures that our digital lives remain intentional and aligned with what matters most to us.

The Difference Between Minimalism and Deprivation

One common misconception about digital minimalism is that it's about depriving ourselves of technology or living a luddite lifestyle. This couldn't be further from the truth. Understanding the difference between minimalism and deprivation is crucial for successfully implementing digital minimalism in our lives.

Minimalism is About Optimization

Digital minimalism is not about using as little technology as possible. Instead, it's about optimizing our technology use to align with our values and goals. It's a deliberate choice to focus on the digital tools and experiences that add the most value to our lives.

For example, a digital minimalist might choose to delete social media apps from their phone to reduce mindless scrolling, but keep a selected few messaging apps to stay connected with close friends and family. This isn't deprivation; it's a strategic choice to optimize their digital experience.

Deprivation Feels Like a Sacrifice; Minimalism Feels Liberating

When we're depriving ourselves, it often feels like a sacrifice. We might feel like we're missing out or that we're forcing ourselves to live with less than we want. This feeling of sacrifice is often unsustainable in the long term.

In contrast, digital minimalism, when done right, feels liberating. By clearing away digital clutter and focusing on what truly matters, we often find that we have more time, more focus, and more satisfaction in our digital lives.

Minimalism is Personalized

Another key difference is that digital minimalism is highly personalized. What constitutes a minimalist approach for one person might look very different for another. It's not about following a prescribed set of rules, but about discovering what works best for you.

For instance, one person might find that they're most productive when they check email only twice a day, while another might need to be more responsive for their job. Digital minimalism allows for these differences, focusing on intersectionality rather than one-size-fits-all solutions.

Minimalism Enhances; Deprivation Restricts

Digital minimalism aims to enhance our lives by helping us use technology more effectively. It's not about restricting our access to useful tools, but about ensuring that the tools we use are truly useful.

For example, a digital minimalist approach to smartphone use might involve:
   - Keeping apps that genuinely improve your life (like meditation apps or educational tools)
   - Removing apps that tend to waste your time or make you feel bad
   - Reorganizing your home screen to prioritize your most valuable apps
   - Setting up app limits or downtime to encourage more intentional use

This approach enhances your smartphone experience by making it more aligned with your goals and values.

Minimalism is Sustainable; Deprivation Often Isn't

Attempts at digital deprivation – like quitting social media cold turkey or swearing off smartphones – often fail because they're too extreme. They don't account for the genuine benefits these technologies can provide when used intentionally.

Digital minimalism, on the other hand, is designed to be sustainable. It's about creating a balanced, intentional relationship with technology that you can maintain over the long term. This sustainability is key to its effectiveness.

Setting Intentional Digital Boundaries

A crucial aspect of digital minimalism is setting intentional boundaries around our technology use. These boundaries help us maintain control over our digital lives and ensure that our technology use aligns with our values and goals. Here are some strategies for setting effective digital boundaries:

1. Define Your Digital Values

Before setting boundaries, it's important to clarify your values when it comes to technology use. Ask yourself:
   - What role do I want technology to play in my life?
   - What are my priorities in terms of how I spend my time?
   - What digital activities bring me the most value?
   - What digital habits do I want to change?

Your answers to these questions will guide your boundary-setting process.

2. Conduct a Digital Audit

Take stock of your current digital habits. This might involve:
   - Tracking your screen time for a week
   - Noting which apps you use most frequently
   - Identifying times of day when you're most likely to engage in mindless digital activity

This audit will help you identify areas where boundaries might be most beneficial.

3. Establish Time-Based Boundaries

One effective way to set digital boundaries is to establish specific times for technology use. This might include:

- Defining "tech-free" times, such as during meals or the first hour after waking up
  - Setting specific times to check email or social media, rather than doing so constantly throughout the day
  - Establishing a "digital sunset" time when you stop using devices before bed

These time-based boundaries can help create space for offline activities and improve your sleep habits.

4. Create Physical Boundaries

Physical boundaries can be powerful in managing our digital lives. Consider:

- Designating certain areas of your home as "tech-free zones" (like the dining room or bedroom)
  - Keeping your phone out of reach while working on important tasks
  - Using a physical alarm clock instead of your phone to avoid late-night scrolling

These physical boundaries can help reduce the temptation of constant connectivity.

5. Implement App Limits and Notifications Management

Most smartphones now offer features to help manage app usage and notifications. Use these tools to:

- Set daily time limits for social media or games
  - Turn off notifications for non-essential apps
  - Use "Do Not Disturb" mode during focused work or family time

Remember, the goal is to be proactive about your app use, rather than reactive to every notification.

6. Practice Digital Sabbaticals

Regular breaks from technology can help reset your relationship with your devices. This might involve:

- Taking a day off from social media each week
  - Having a "no phones" rule during certain activities or outings
  - Trying a longer digital detox during vacations

These sabbaticals can help you appreciate both the benefits of technology and the joy of being unplugged.

7. Curate Your Digital Inputs

Be intentional about what you allow into your digital space:

- Follow accounts that don't add value to your life
  - Be selective about which news sources you follow
  - Curate your email subscriptions regularly

Remember, what you pay attention to shapes your thoughts and experiences. Be choosy about your digital inputs.

8. Establish Communication Norms

Set expectations with others about your digital availability:

- Let colleagues know your email checking schedule
    - Establish response time expectations for different communication channels
    - Communicate your "off hours" to respect work-life boundaries

Clear communication can prevent misunderstandings and reduce the pressure to be always available.

9. Use Technology to Support Your Boundaries

Ironically, technology itself can be a powerful ally in setting digital boundaries. Consider using:

- Apps that block distracting websites during work hours
    - Screen time tracking apps to monitor your progress
    - Digital well being features built into your devices

These tools can provide accountability and support as you implement your digital boundaries.

10. Regularly Reassess and Adjust

Your digital boundaries should evolve as your life and needs change. Regularly ask yourself:

- Are these boundaries still serving me well?
    - Have new digital challenges emerged that I need to address?
    - Are there areas where I can be even more intentional with my technology use?

Be willing to experiment and adjust your boundaries as needed.

11. Practice Self-Compassion

Setting and maintaining digital boundaries isn't always easy. There will likely be times when you slip up or struggle. That's okay. Treat these moments as learning opportunities rather than failures.

Remember, the goal of digital minimalism isn't perfection, but progress towards a more intentional relationship with technology.

In conclusion, digital minimalism offers a thoughtful approach to technology use in our increasingly connected world. By understanding its core philosophies, recognizing the difference between minimalism and deprivation, and setting intentional digital boundaries, we can create a digital life that enhances rather than detracts from our overall well-being.

Digital minimalism isn't about rejecting the amazing capabilities that modern technology offers. Instead, it's about harnessing those capabilities in a way that aligns with our values, supports our goals, and allows us to live more fully both online and offline. As we move forward, we'll explore how to put these principles into practice, creating a digital life that's less cluttered, more intentional, and ultimately more satisfying.

The Benefits of a Minimalist Digital Life

As we navigate our increasingly digital world, the practice of digital minimalism offers a path to a more intentional and fulfilling relationship with technology. But what exactly can we gain from adopting this approach? In this chapter, we'll explore the myriad benefits that a minimalist digital life can bring, focusing on three key areas: improved focus and productivity, enhanced creativity and problem-solving, and better work-life balance and personal relationships.

Improved Focus and Productivity

One of the most immediate and noticeable benefits of digital minimalism is the improvement in our ability to focus and, consequently, our overall productivity. Here's how a minimalist digital life can enhance these crucial aspects of our daily lives:

1. Reduced Digital Distractions

By consciously limiting our digital inputs and creating intentional boundaries around our technology use, we significantly reduce the number of distractions competing for our attention. This reduction in digital noise allows us to focus more deeply on the task at hand, whether it's work-related or personal.

For instance, turning off non-essential notifications or designating specific times for checking emails and social media can create uninterrupted blocks of time for focused work. A study by the University of California, Irvine, found that it takes an average of 23 minutes and 15 seconds to fully refocus after an interruption. By minimizing these interruptions, we can potentially save hours of productive time each day.

2. Improved Attention Span

Constant exposure to quick-hit digital content, like social media posts or short videos, can train our brains to expect instant gratification and struggle with longer periods of focus. Digital minimalism encourages us to engage in more sustained, focused activities, which can help rebuild and strengthen our attention span over time.

Dr. Cal Newport, in his book "Deep Work," argues that the ability to focus without distraction on a cognitively demanding task is becoming increasingly rare and increasingly valuable in our economy. By practicing digital minimalism, we cultivate this valuable skill.

3. Enhanced Single-Tasking Ability

While multitasking is often glorified in our digital age, research consistently shows that it's ineffective and can even be harmful to our cognitive abilities. Digital minimalism promotes single-tasking – focusing on one task at a time – which has been proven to be far more effective.

A study published in the Journal of Experimental Psychology found that participants who multi tasked took up to 40% longer to complete tasks and made more mistakes compared to those who single-tasked. By embracing digital minimalism, we can break free from the multitasking myth and become more efficient in our work.

4. Increased Mindfulness and Presence

Digital minimalism encourages us to be more present in our daily lives, rather than constantly dividing our attention between the physical world and our digital devices. This increased mindfulness can lead to greater engagement with our work, resulting in higher quality output and increased job satisfaction.

5. Improved Time Management

When we're not constantly reactive to digital stimuli, we can be more proactive in how we manage our time. Digital minimalism often involves planning our technology use, which can extend to better overall time management skills. We become more aware of how we spend our time and can allocate it more effectively to tasks that truly matter.

6. Reduced Decision Fatigue

Our digital lives often require us to make countless small decisions throughout the day – which email to respond to first, which notification to check, which piece of content to engage with. These decisions, while seemingly insignificant, can accumulate and lead to decision fatigue, reducing our capacity to make important decisions later in the day.

By streamlining our digital lives, we reduce the number of micro-decisions we need to make, preserving our decision-making energy for more important matters.

Enhanced Creativity and Problem-Solving

Beyond improving focus and productivity, digital minimalism can also boost our creative capabilities and problem-solving skills. Here's how:

1. Creating Space for Reflection

In our always-on digital culture, we rarely give our minds the chance to wander or reflect. Yet, this mental downtime is crucial for creativity and problem-solving. Digital minimalism creates pockets of boredom and quietude in our lives, which can be incredibly fertile ground for new ideas and insights.

Renowned physicist Richard Feynman once said, "The pleasure of finding things out is the essence of creativity." By stepping away from the constant input of digital information, we give ourselves the opportunity to make new connections and discoveries.

2. Reducing Information Overload

While the internet provides us with a wealth of information at our fingertips, this constant influx of data can actually hinder our creative thinking. When our minds are cluttered with excessive information, it becomes harder to think originally or see problems from new angles.

Digital minimalism encourages us to be more selective about our information inputs, allowing us to focus on depth rather than breadth. This curated approach to information can lead to deeper understanding and more creative insights.

3. Enhancing Divergent Thinking

Divergent thinking – the ability to generate creative ideas by exploring many possible solutions – is a key component of creativity. However, our digital habits often promote convergent thinking, where we quickly search for the "right" answer online.

By reducing our reliance on quick digital searches, digital minimalism can enhance our capacity for divergent thinking. We're more likely to sit with a problem, approach it from multiple angles, and come up with novel solutions.

4. Improving Concentration for Complex Problem-Solving

Complex problems often require sustained, focused thought to solve. The distraction-free periods promoted by digital minimalism provide the perfect environment for tackling these challenging issues. Without the constant pull of digital notifications, we can dive deep into problems and stay with them until we reach a breakthrough.

5. Fostering Real-World Experiences

Creativity doesn't happen in a vacuum – it's often sparked by our experiences in the real world. Digital minimalism encourages us to engage more fully with our physical environment and the people around us, providing new stimuli and perspectives that can fuel creative thinking.

Steve Jobs famously said, "Creativity is just connecting things." By diversifying our experiences beyond the digital realm, we give ourselves more "things" to connect, enhancing our creative potential.

6. Enhancing Cognitive Flexibility

Constant digital stimulation can create rigid thinking patterns, where we become accustomed to quick, surface-level engagement with ideas. Digital minimalism, by contrast, can enhance our cognitive flexibility – our ability to adapt our thinking and behavior in response to new situations.

This improved cognitive flexibility is crucial for both creativity and problem-solving, allowing us to approach challenges from multiple perspectives and adapt our strategies as needed.

Better Work-Life Balance and Personal Relationships

Perhaps one of the most significant benefits of digital minimalism is its positive impact on our work-life balance and personal relationships. Here's how adopting a minimalist digital lifestyle can enhance these crucial aspects of our lives:

1. Clearer Boundaries Between Work and Personal Life

In our always-connected world, the lines between work and personal life have become increasingly blurred. We check work emails at the dinner table, respond to messages late at night, and never truly "leave" the office. Digital minimalism encourages us to set clear boundaries around our technology use, which can translate into clearer boundaries between our professional and personal lives.

For example, implementing a "digital sunset" – a time after which we don't engage with work-related digital communications – can help us fully disconnect from work and be present with our families or engage in personal activities. This separation can lead to reduced stress, better rest, and increased job satisfaction.

2. Increased Quality Time with Loved Ones

When we're constantly distracted by our devices, we're not fully present with the people around us. Digital minimalism promotes putting away our devices during social interactions, leading to more meaningful conversations and stronger connections.

A study published in the journal Psychology of Popular Media Culture found that the mere presence of a phone during a conversation (even if it's not being used) can reduce the quality of the interaction and the level of empathy between participants. By practicing digital minimalism, we can create more opportunities for deep, meaningful interactions with our loved ones.

3. Improved Emotional Well-being

Excessive use of social media and other digital platforms has been linked to increased rates of anxiety, depression, and loneliness. By reducing our digital consumption, we can mitigate these negative effects and improve our overall emotional well-being.

Moreover, the practice of digital minimalism often leads to increased self-reflection and mindfulness, which are associated with better mental health outcomes. When we're not constantly distracted by digital noise, we have more opportunity to check in with ourselves, process our emotions, and engage in activities that truly bring us joy and fulfillment.

4. Enhanced Real-World Social Skills

As we spend more time engaging in face-to-face interactions rather than digital communications, we naturally hone our real-world social skills. These skills – reading body language, engaging in active listening, navigating complex social situations – are crucial for building and maintaining strong relationships, both personal and professional.

5. More Time for Hobbies and Personal Growth

Digital minimalism frees up time that we might have previously spent scrolling through social media or binge-watching TV shows. This newfound time can be redirected towards hobbies, learning new skills, or engaging in personal development activities.

Pursuing interests outside of work not only contributes to personal fulfill-ment but can also make us more well-rounded individuals and professionals. It can provide new perspectives that enhance our work performance and give us topics for meaningful conversations in our personal relationships.

6. Reduced FOMO (Fear of Missing Out)

The constant stream of information on social media can fuel a fear of missing out, leading to anxiety and dissatisfaction with our own lives. Digital minimalism helps us break free from this cycle by encouraging us to focus on our own experiences rather than constantly comparing ourselves to others.

As we become more present in our own lives and less concerned with curating our online presence, we often find greater contentment and appreciation for our real-world experiences and relationships.

7. Improved Sleep Quality

The blue light emitted by our devices can interfere with our sleep patterns, and the stimulation from late-night scrolling or email checking can make it difficult to wind down. Digital minimalism often involves creating tech-free periods before bedtime, which can lead to improved sleep quality.

Better sleep doesn't just make us feel more rested – it has cascading benefits for our mood, cognitive function, and overall health, all of which contribute to better work performance and more positive personal relationships.

8. More Authentic Relationships

Social media often encourages us to present a curated, idealized version of our lives. This can create a sense of disconnection and in authenticity in our relationships. By stepping back from this digital performance, we can focus on building more authentic connections based on real, shared experiences.

9. Increased Empathy and Understanding

When we're not constantly bombarded with information and opinions from our digital networks, we have more mental space to truly listen to and understand the people around us. This can lead to increased empathy and stronger, more supportive relationships.

A study published in the journal Computers in Human Behavior found that people who had face-to-face conversations, as opposed to digital interactions, reported higher levels of bonding and empathy. By prioritizing in-person interactions, digital minimalism can help us build deeper, more empathetic relationships.

10. Improved Conflict Resolution Skills

In the digital world, it's easy to misinterpret tone, avoid difficult conversations, or react impulsively. By encouraging more face-to-face communication, digital minimalism can help us develop better conflict resolution skills. We learn to read non-verbal cues, engage in real-time problem-solving, and navigate complex emotional terrain more effectively.

In conclusion, the benefits of adopting a minimalist digital life are far-reaching and profound. From sharpening our focus and boosting our productivity to enhancing our creative capabilities and nurturing our personal relationships, digital minimalism offers a path to a more balanced, fulfilling life in the digital age.

It's important to note that these benefits don't occur overnight. Like any significant lifestyle change, digital minimalism requires commitment and practice. There may be initial discomfort as we break old habits and establish new ones. However, as we persist, we often find that the benefits far outweigh the temporary challenges.

Moreover, digital minimalism isn't about completely eschewing technology. Rather, it's about using technology more intentionally to support our goals and values. The aim is to harness the incredible power of digital tools while mitigating their potential downsides.

As we move forward in our exploration of digital minimalism, keep these benefits in mind. They serve not only as motivation for embracing this approach but also as a road map for the positive changes we can expect to see in our lives. In the following chapters, we'll delve into practical strategies for implementing digital minimalism and overcoming common obstacles, always with an eye toward realizing these trans formative benefits in our own lives.

Overcoming Obstacles to Digital Minimalism

While the benefits of digital minimalism are numerous and compelling, the path to achieving a more intentional relationship with technology is not without its challenges. In this chapter, we'll explore some of the most common obstacles people face when attempting to embrace digital minimalism and provide practical strategies for overcoming them.

Fear of Missing Out (FOMO) and How to Combat It

Fear of Missing Out, commonly known as FOMO, is one of the most significant psychological barriers to adopting a minimalist digital lifestyle. In our hyper-connected world, the fear that we might be missing important information, social opportunities, or experiences can drive compulsive checking of devices and social media platforms.

Understanding FOMO

FOMO is more than just a trendy acronym; it's a real psychological phenomenon. A study published in the journal "Computers in Human Behavior" defines FOMO as "a pervasive apprehension that others might be having rewarding experiences from which one is absent."

This fear is often amplified by social media, where we're constantly exposed to curated highlights of others' lives. The more we engage with these platforms, the more we fear we're missing out when we're not connected.

Strategies to Combat FOMO

1. Practice Mindfulness: Mindfulness techniques can help you stay present and appreciate your current experiences rather than worrying about what you might be missing. Try mindfulness meditation apps or simple breathing exercises.

2. Cultivate Gratitude: Regularly practicing gratitude can shift your focus from what you might be missing to what you already have. Consider keeping a gratitude journal where you write down three things you're thankful for each day.

3. Re frame Your Perspective: Remember that social media often presents a highlight reel, not reality. Remind yourself that what you see online is usually a carefully curated version of people's lives.

4. Set Boundaries: Establish specific times for checking social media or news, rather than constantly dipping in and out. This can help reduce the anxiety of potentially missing something.

5. Create JOMO (Joy of Missing Out): Actively appreciate the benefits of disconnecting. Enjoy the peace of a quiet evening without digital distraction, or the depth of a face-to-face conversation without interruptions.

6. Curate Your Digital Inputs: Be selective about who you follow and what content you consume. Follow accounts that trigger FOMO and focus on those that inspire and uplift you.

7. Engage in Offline Activities: Invest time in hobbies, exercise, or social

activities that don't involve digital devices. This can help you build a fulfilling offline life that reduces the appeal of constant digital connection.

Real-Life Application

Sarah, a marketing professional, found herself constantly checking social media out of fear of missing important industry news or networking opportunities. To combat this, she set specific times for professional social media use, curated her follows to focus on key industry leaders, and set up targeted alerts for truly important news. She also joined a local marketing group that met in person monthly, providing valuable face-to-face networking opportunities. These strategies helped her stay informed without the constant anxiety of potentially missing out.

Breaking the Dopamine Feedback Loop

Our digital devices and apps are designed to be addictive, leveraging the brain's reward system to keep us engaged. Understanding and breaking this dopamine feedback loop is crucial for embracing digital minimalism.

Understanding the Dopamine Feedback Loop

Dopamine is a neurotransmitter associated with pleasure and reward. When we receive a notification or a "like" on social media, our brains release a small amount of dopamine, creating a pleasurable sensation. This creates a feedback loop: we check our phones or social media accounts in anticipation of this reward, reinforcing the behavior.

Dr. Anna Lembke, a psychiatrist and author of "Dopamine Nation," describes this as a "dopamine deficit state." The more we engage in these behaviors, the more dopamine we need to feel the same level of pleasure, leading to compulsive checking and scrolling.

Strategies to Break the Loop

1. Create Physical Distance: Keep your phone out of reach, especially during focused work or family time. The extra effort required to check it can help break the automatic nature of the behavior.

2. Use Gray scale Mode: Many smartphones have a setting that turns the display to gray scale. This can make the device less visually appealing and reduce the dopamine hit from colorful app icons and notifications.

3. Turn Off Push Notifications: Disable notifications for non-essential apps. This reduces the external triggers that prompt you to check your device.

4. Implement the Two-Minute Rule: If an urge to check your phone or a specific app arises, wait two minutes before acting on it. Often, the urge will pass.

5. Find Alternative Dopamine Sources: Engage in activities that provide a natural dopamine boost, such as exercise, completing a task, or spending time in nature.

6. Practice Delayed Gratification: Set specific times for checking social media or emails, and stick to them. This helps retrain your brain to be comfortable with waiting for the dopamine hit.

7. Use Apps to Your Advantage: Ironically, there are apps designed to help you use your phone less. Consider using screen time tracking apps or apps that block certain features after a set amount of use.

8. Engage in Digital Detox Periods: Regular periods of complete digital disconnection can help reset your dopamine sensitivity.

Real-Life Application

Mike, a software developer, found himself compulsively checking his phone throughout the day. To break this habit, he first turned off all non-essential notifications. He then installed an app that locked him out of social media apps after 30 minutes of daily use. To replace the dopamine hit from social media, he started taking short walks during his work breaks and picked up a neglected hobby of playing guitar. Over time, he found his urge to constantly check his phone diminished, and he felt more present and focused both at work and at home.

Dealing with Work and Social Expectations

In our always-on digital culture, there's often an expectation of constant availability, both in professional and social contexts. This can make it challenging to set boundaries and embrace digital minimalism.

Understanding the Challenge

The expectation of immediate response to emails, messages, and social media interactions can create significant stress and make it difficult to disconnect. This is compounded by the blurring of lines between work and personal life, especially with the rise of remote work.

A study by the American Psychological Association found that 86% of Americans constantly or often check their emails, texts, and social media accounts. This constant checking is often driven by a fear of missing important information or appearing unresponsive to colleagues or friends.

Strategies for Managing Expectations

1. Communicate Your Boundaries: Clearly communicate your digital habits to colleagues, friends, and family. Let them know when you'll be available and when you'll be offline.

2. Set Auto-Responders: Use email auto-responders to manage expectations about your response time. For example: "I check emails twice daily at 10 AM and 4 PM. For urgent matters, please call..."

3. Establish 'Off-Hours' Protocols: If you're in a leadership position, set clear guidelines about after-hours communication. If you're not, discuss with your manager about establishing such protocols.

4. Use 'Do Not Disturb' Features: Most smartphones have features that allow you to silence notifications during certain hours or from specific apps.

5. Batch Process Communications: Instead of responding to messages as they come in, set specific times to check and respond to emails, texts, and social media interactions.

6. Lead by Example: If you're in a position of influence, model healthy digital habits. This can help shift the culture in your workplace or social circle.

7. Educate Others on the Benefits: Share information about the benefits of digital minimalism with colleagues and friends. This can help create a supportive environment for your efforts.

8. Use Technology to Support Boundaries: Utilize features like delayed send for emails or scheduled posts for social media to maintain a presence without being constantly online.

9. Prioritize Face-to-Face Interactions: When possible, opt for in-person meetings or phone calls over prolonged digital communications. This can often lead to more efficient and meaningful interactions.

Handling Specific Situations

In the Workplace:

1. Manage Up: Discuss your productivity strategies, including digital minimalism, with your manager. Frame it in terms of how it will benefit your work performance.

2. Set Realistic Response Times: Establish clear expectations about response times for different types of communication (e.g., instant for urgent matters, within 24 hours for standard emails).

3. Use Status Updates: If your workplace uses communication tools like Slack, use status updates to indicate when you're in focused work mode and not immediately available.

4. Negotiate Flexibility: If possible, negotiate flexible working hours that allow for periods of uninterrupted focus time.

In Social Settings:

1. Be Present: When spending time with friends or family, make a point of putting your phone away. This sets an example and encourages others to do the same.

2. Explain Your Choices: If friends comment on your reduced social media presence, explain your decision to embrace digital minimalism. Many may be supportive or even inspired to try it themselves.

3. Suggest Alternative Ways to Connect: If you're reducing time on social platforms, suggest other ways to stay in touch, like regular phone calls or in-person meetups.

4. Create Phone-Free Social Events: Organize gatherings where everyone agrees to keep phones put away, promoting more engaged, present interactions.

Real-Life Application

Emily, a marketing manager, found herself constantly stressed by the expectation to be always available. She decided to implement several strategies to manage these expectations:

1. She communicated to her team that she would be checking emails three times a day and provided her phone number for truly urgent matters.

2. She set up an auto-responded explaining her email checking schedule and expected response times.

3. For her direct reports, she made it clear that she didn't expect responses to emails sent after hours until the next workday.

4. She started using the 'Do Not Disturb' feature on her phone after 8 PM and before 8 AM.

5. In team meetings, she discussed the benefits of focused work time and encouraged others to establish similar boundaries.

6. For friends, she explained her new approach to digital communication and suggested alternative ways to stay in touch, like monthly dinner gatherings.

Initially, Emily faced some resistance and anxiety about these changes. However, over time, her colleagues and friends adapted to her new habits. She found that not only did her stress levels decrease, but her productivity at work improved, and her social interactions became more meaningful.

Overcoming obstacles to digital minimalism is an ongoing process that requires patience, persistence, and a willingness to challenge societal norms. It's important to remember that these changes don't happen overnight. It's okay to start small and gradually expand your digital minimalism practices.

As you work to combat FOMO, break dopamine feedback loops, and manage work and social expectations, keep in mind the benefits you're working towards: improved focus, enhanced creativity, better relationships, and a greater sense of control over your time and attention.

Also, remember that digital minimalism isn't about completely eliminating technology from your life. It's about being intentional with your digital usage, ensuring that technology serves your goals and values rather than distracting from them.

Lastly, be kind to yourself in this process. There will likely be setbacks and moments of struggle. Treat these as learning opportunities rather than failures. Each step you take towards a more intentional relationship with technology is a step towards a more focused, balanced, and fulfilling life.

In the next chapters, we'll explore practical strategies for implementing digital minimalism in various aspects of your life, from decluttering your devices to creating sustainable digital routines. Remember, the goal is progress, not perfection, in your journey towards a more mindful

Decluttering Your Devices

I n our journey towards digital minimalism, one of the most impact steps
we can take is decluttering our devices. Our smartphones, computers,
and other digital tools are the gateways to our digital lives, and by
streamlining these devices, we can significantly reduce digital noise and create
a more intentional digital environment. In this chapter, we'll explore practical
strategies for decluttering your smartphone, organizing your computer, and
managing multiple devices effectively.

Streamlining Your Smartphone: Apps, Notifications, and Settings

Our smartphones are often the biggest source of digital clutter in our lives.
They're with us constantly, buzzing with notifications and filled with apps
vying for our attention. Here's how to transform your smartphone from a
source of distraction into a tool for intentional living:

1. Conduct an App Audit

Begin by reviewing all the apps on your phone. For each app, ask yourself:
- When was the last time I used this app?
- Does this app align with my values and goals?
- Is this app essential, or just nice to have?

Be ruthless in your assessment. If an app doesn't provide significant value or
hasn't been used in the last month, consider deleting it. Remember, you can

always re-download an app if you find you truly need it later.

2. Organize Remaining Apps

For the apps you decide to keep:
- Group similar apps into folders (e.g., "Productivity", "Communication", "Entertainment")
- Move your most essential apps to the home screen and less frequently used apps to secondary screens
- Consider using a minimalist launcher (for Android) or rearranging your home screen (for iOS) to reduce visual clutter

3. Tame Your Notifications

Notifications are one of the biggest sources of digital distraction. To regain control:
- Turn off notifications for all non-essential apps
- For essential apps, customize notifications to only alert you for truly important information
- Use "Do Not Disturb" mode during focused work times or overnight
- Consider enabling "Scheduled Summary" (iOS) or "Notification History" (Android) to batch non-urgent notifications

4. Optimize Your Settings

Take advantage of built-in features designed to help you use your phone more mindfully:
- Enable gray scale mode to make your phone less visually appealing during certain hours
- Use "Screen Time" (iOS) or "Digital Well being" (Android) to set app time limits
- Enable "Night Shift" (iOS) or "Night Light" (Android) to reduce blue light exposure in the evening

- Customize your lock screen to show only essential information

5. Declutter Your Home Screen

Your home screen should be a calming space that encourages intentional use:
- Limit the number of apps on your home screen to only the most essential
- Use a simple, calming wallpaper
- Remove widgets that aren't providing significant value
- Consider using a minimalist icon pack to reduce visual noise

6. Clean Up Your Photos and Messages

Don't forget about the clutter that accumulates in your photos and messages:
- Regularly delete unnecessary photos and videos
- Back up important media to the cloud, then remove them from your device
- Delete old conversations and clear out your message inbox

7. Streamline Your Email on Mobile

Email can be a major source of digital clutter:
- Unsubscribe from newsletters you no longer read
- Set up filters to automatically sort incoming emails
- Consider using a dedicated email app that supports "batching" to check emails at set times

Organizing Your Computer: Files, Programs, and Desktop

Our computers often contain years of accumulated digital clutter. Here's how to bring order to your digital workspace:

1. Declutter Your Desktop

A cluttered desktop can be visually overwhelming and make it harder to focus:
- Remove all files and shortcuts from your desktop
- Create a simple folder structure on your desktop for temporary files (e.g., "To Sort", "Current Projects")
- Use a minimalist wallpaper to reduce visual distraction

2. Organize Your File System

An organized file system makes it easier to find what you need and reduces mental clutter:
- Create a logical folder structure (e.g., Documents, Photos, Projects)
- Use descriptive, consistent file names
- Regularly delete or archive old files you no longer need
- Consider using a file naming convention (e.g., YYYY-MM-DD_Project Name_File Name)

3. Clean Up Your Programs

Just like with smartphone apps, it's easy to accumulate unnecessary programs:
- Uninstall programs you no longer use
- For programs you use infrequently, consider using web-based alternatives
- Disable programs that automatically start with your computer unless absolutely necessary

4. Optimize Your Browser

For many of us, the web browser is our most-used program:
- Declutter your bookmarks, keeping only those you regularly use
- Organize remaining bookmarks into folders
- Clear your browser history and cache regularly
- Consider using extensions that block ads and reduce visual clutter

5. Manage Your Email

Email can be a major source of digital clutter on computers:
- Set up folders or labels to organize emails
- Use filters to automatically sort incoming emails
- Regularly archive or delete old emails
- Aim for "Inbox Zero" or a simplified inbox management system

6. Streamline Your Cloud Storage

Cloud storage can easily become a dumping ground for digital files:
- Organize your cloud storage using a similar structure to your local files
- Regularly review and delete unnecessary files
- Use selective sync to only keep essential files on your local machine

7. Create a Digital Filing System

For important documents:
- Scan physical documents and save them as searchable PDFs
- Create a logical folder structure for digital documents
- Use consistent naming conventions for easy searching
- Regularly review and purge unnecessary documents

Managing Multiple Devices: Syncing and Consistency

In today's digital ecosystem, most of us use multiple devices. Here's how to maintain consistency and reduce redundancy across your devices:

1. Choose a Primary Cloud Service

Select one cloud service (e.g., Google Drive, i Cloud, Dropbox) as your primary storage and syncing solution:
- Use this service to sync important files across all your devices

- Ensure all your devices are set up to automatically backup to this service

2. Implement Cross-Device App Consistency

For apps you use across multiple devices:
- Use the same apps across devices where possible
- Ensure settings and preferences are consistent across devices
- Use cloud syncing features to keep data consistent (e.g., browser bookmarks, notes)

3. Utilize Universal Clipboard and Han doff Features

If you're in the Apple ecosystem, take advantage of features like Universal Clipboard and Handoff:
- These features allow you to start a task on one device and seamlessly continue on another
- For non-Apple users, consider apps like Push Bullet that offer similar functionality

4. Streamline Your Password Management

Use a password manager to maintain consistent and secure access across all devices:
- Choose a reputable password manager (e.g., Last Pass, 1 Password)
- Use it to generate and store strong, unique passwords for all your accounts
- Ensure the password manager is installed and synced across all your devices

5. Maintain Consistent Notification Settings

To avoid notification overload:
- Aim for consistent notification settings across devices
- Consider disabling redundant notifications (e.g., you probably don't need

email notifications on both your phone and computer)

6. Implement a Consistent File Structure

Use the same file organization structure across all your devices:
- This makes it easier to find files regardless of which device you're using
- Use your cloud service to maintain this consistent structure

7. Regular Cross-Device Cleanup

Schedule regular "digital cleanup" sessions:
- Review and delete unnecessary files across all devices
- Ensure your apps and software are up-to-date on all devices
- Check that your syncing and backup systems are working correctly

8. Use Device-Specific Features Intentionally

While consistency is important, also leverage the unique strengths of each device:
- Use your smartphone for on-the-go tasks and quick captures
- Use your computer for deep work and complex tasks
- Use tablets or e-readers for distraction-free reading

9. Implement Cross-Device Focus Modes

Many operating systems now offer focus or do-not-disturb modes:
- Set up these modes consistently across your devices
- Use them to create periods of uninterrupted focus, regardless of which device you're using

10. Consider Digital Minimalism Across Devices

Apply the principles of digital minimalism to all your devices:

- Aim for a minimalist aesthetic on all devices
- Keep only essential apps and files on each device
- Regularly question whether you need certain apps or files on multiple devices

Practical Tips for Implementation

Decluttering your devices can seem overwhelming, but remember that it's a process. Here are some tips to make it more manageable:

1. Start Small: Begin with one device or one area (like your smartphone's home screen) and build from there.

2. Set Aside Dedicated Time: Schedule specific times for digital decluttering, treating it as an important task.

3. Use the "One In, One Out" Rule: When you add a new app or file, remove an old one to maintain balance.

4. Regular Maintenance: Set reminders for regular "digital cleanups" to prevent clutter from accumulating again.

5. Involve Others: If you share devices with family members, involve them in the decluttering process to ensure everyone's needs are met.

6. Be Patient with Yourself: Changing digital habits takes time. Be patient and celebrate small victories along the way.

7. Reassess Regularly: Your needs may change over time. Regularly reassess your digital setup and adjust as necessary.

Decluttering your devices is a powerful step towards digital minimalism. By streamlining your smartphone, organizing your computer, and managing multiple devices effectively, you create a digital environment that supports focus, productivity, and intentional living.

Remember, the goal isn't to strip your digital life bare, but to curate a digital environment that truly serves you. As you go through this process, continually ask yourself: "Does this app/file/notification add value to my life?" If the answer is no, let it go.

In the next chapters, we'll explore how to apply these decluttering principles to specific areas of your digital life, such as email management and social media use. Each step you take brings you closer to a more intentional, less cluttered digital existence.

Taming Your Inbox

I n our digital age, email has become a central part of both our professional and personal lives. However, for many, it's also a significant source of stress and digital clutter. An overflowing inbox can lead to missed important messages, wasted time, and a constant feeling of being overwhelmed. In this chapter, we'll explore effective strategies for managing your email, unsubscribing from unnecessary communications, and achieving the coveted state of "Inbox Zero."

Email Management Techniques

Effective email management is crucial for maintaining productivity and reducing digital stress. Here are some techniques to help you take control of your inbox:

1. Implement the "Two-Minute Rule"

Productivity expert David Allen recommends the "Two-Minute Rule": If an email can be dealt with in two minutes or less, handle it immediately. This prevents small tasks from piling up and becoming overwhelming.

- Read the email
    - Decide if it can be handled in two minutes or less
    - If yes, respond, file, or delete it immediately
    - If no, add it to your to-do list or schedule time to deal with it later

2. Use the "Four D's" Method

For emails that require more than two minutes, apply the "Four D's" method:

- Delete: If it's not important or relevant, delete it immediately.
    - Do: If it's urgent and important, do it now.
    - Delegate: If someone else can handle it better, forward it to them.
    - Defer: If it's important but not urgent, schedule time to deal with it later.

3. Create an Email Schedule

Rather than checking your email constantly throughout the day, set specific times for email management:

- Check emails at set intervals (e.g., 9 AM, 1 PM, and 4 PM)
    - Turn off email notifications outside of these times
    - Communicate your email schedule to colleagues and clients to manage expectations

4. Use Folders or Labels Effectively

Organize your emails into folders or labels for easy reference:

- Create broad categories (e.g., "Projects," "Personal," "Finance")
    - Use sub-folders for more specific categorization
    - Consider using a numbering system for prioritization (e.g., "1-Urgent," "2-This Week," "3-This Month")

5. Employ the "OHIO" Principle

OHIO stands for "Only Handle It Once." When you open an email, make a decision about it immediately:

- Respond if necessary
  - File it in the appropriate folder
  - Delete it if it's not needed
  - Add any required actions to your to-do list

6. Utilize Email Templates

For frequently sent emails, create templates to save time:

- Draft responses for common inquiries
  - Create templates for regular updates or reports
  - Use your email client's canned response or template feature

7. Practice Good Email Etiquette

Improve the efficiency of your email communications:

- Use clear, specific subject lines
  - Keep emails concise and to the point
  - Use bullet points for easy scanning
  - Clearly state any required actions or responses

8. Regularly Archive Old Emails

Prevent your inbox from becoming a storage unit:

- Regularly move old emails to an archive folder
  - Set up automatic archiving for emails older than a certain date
  - Use your email client's archive feature to keep your inbox current

Unsubscribing and Filtering Strategies

A significant portion of email clutter comes from newsletters, promotional emails, and other subscriptions that we've accumulated over time. Here's how to cut through this clutter:

1. Conduct a Subscription Audit

Review all the emails you receive over a week or two:

- Identify recurring newsletters or promotional emails
    - Assess which ones you actually read and find valuable
    - Make a list of subscriptions to keep and those to unsubscribe from

2. Unsubscribe Systematically

For emails you no longer want to receive:

- Look for an "Unsubscribe" link, usually at the bottom of the email
    - Use a service like Unroll.me to bulk unsubscribe from multiple lists
    - For stubborn senders, set up a filter to automatically delete their emails

3. Use the "Plus Sign" Trick for Future Subscriptions

When signing up for new services:

- Use your email+category@domain.com (e.g., johndoe+shopping@gmail.com)
    - This allows you to easily filter or unsubscribe from specific categories later

4. Create Smart Filters

Use your email client's filtering capabilities to automatically sort incoming mail:

- Create filters based on sender, subject line, or content

- Automatically move newsletters to a "Reading" folder
- Send non-urgent notifications to a "Low Priority" folder

5. Use a Dedicated Email for Subscriptions

Consider using a separate email address for online shopping and subscriptions:

- This keeps your primary inbox cleaner
  - You can check this email address less frequently

6. Implement a "Waiting Room" for New Subscriptions

For new subscriptions:

- Create a "New Subscriptions" folder
  - Set up a filter to send all new subscription emails to this folder for a month
  - After a month, decide whether to keep the subscription or unsubscribe

7. Regularly Review and Update Filters

As your email habits change:

- Review your filters every few months
  - Update or delete filters that are no longer relevant
  - Create new filters for emerging patterns in your email

8. Use Third-Party Services Wisely

Consider using services that help manage subscriptions:

- SaneBox for intelligent email sorting
  - Clean Email for bulk unsubscribing and automation rules

- Remember to review the privacy policies of these services before use

Achieving and Maintaining Inbox Zero

"Inbox Zero" is a rigorous approach to email management aimed at keeping the inbox empty, or almost empty, at all times. While it may seem daunting, with the right strategies, it's an achievable goal that can significantly reduce email-related stress.

1. Start with a Clean Slate

Begin your Inbox Zero journey with a fresh start:

- Create a new folder called "To Process"
    - Move all existing emails into this folder
    - Commit to processing these over time, but start with an empty inbox

2. Process New Emails Immediately

As new emails arrive:

- Decide immediately what action is required
    - Use the "Two-Minute Rule" and "Four D's" method
    - The goal is to keep emails from accumulating in your inbox

3. Use the "Touch-It-Once" Principle

Similar to the OHIO principle:

- When you open an email, deal with it completely
    - Avoid reading emails and then marking them as unread

4. Set Up an Effective Folder System

Create a simple, intuitive folder system:

- "Action Required" for emails you need to act on
    - "Waiting For" for emails where you're awaiting a response
    - "Archive" for emails you may need to reference later

5. Use Your Calendar Effectively

For emails that require action but not immediately:

- Create a calendar event for the task
    - Include relevant email information in the event details
    - Archive the email once it's on your calendar

6. Embrace the "Archive" Button

Don't be afraid to archive emails:

- If you've dealt with an email, archive it
    - Most email clients have powerful search functions to find archived emails
    - This keeps your inbox clear without losing information

7. Implement a Regular "Email Power Hour"

Schedule dedicated time for email management:

- Set aside an hour each day (or every few days) for focused email processing
    - Use this time to clear out your inbox and maintain Inbox Zero

8. Use Email Client Features to Your Advantage

Many email clients have features that support Inbox Zero:

- Gmail's "Multiple Inboxes" for different action categories
  - Outlook's "Focused Inbox" to separate important emails
  - Apple Mail's "VIP" feature for priority senders

9. Practice the "Five Sentences or Less" Rule

When responding to emails:

- Aim to keep responses to five sentences or less
  - For longer responses, consider a phone call or meeting instead
  - This saves time and encourages clearer communication

10. Regularly Reassess and Adjust Your System

Inbox Zero is not a one-time achievement but an ongoing process:

- Regularly review your email management system
  - Adjust your folders, filters, and habits as needed
  - Be willing to experiment with new techniques and tools

11. Manage Expectations

Communicate your email habits to others:

- Let colleagues know your email checking schedule
  - Use an email signature that explains your response policy
  - Set up an auto-responded for times when you're not available

12. Don't Aim for Perfection

Remember that Inbox Zero is a tool, not a goal in itself:

- It's okay if your inbox isn't always at zero

- The aim is to reduce email-related stress and increase productivity
- Be flexible and adjust the system to work for you

Practical Implementation Tips

Implementing these email management strategies can seem overwhelming at first. Here are some tips to make the process more manageable:

1. Start Small: Begin with one technique at a time. For example, start with the "Two-Minute Rule" for a week before introducing another strategy.

2. Set Realistic Goals: If you're starting with thousands of emails, aim to reduce by a certain number each day rather than tackling everything at once.

3. Use Technology to Your Advantage: Explore the features of your email client. Many have built-in tools for sorting, filtering, and managing emails effectively.

4. Create Email-Free Time: Designate certain times of day as email-free to focus on deep work or personal time.

5. Educate Your Network: Let colleagues, friends, and family know about your new email habits. This can help manage their expectations and even inspire them to adopt similar practices.

6. Review and Refine: Regularly assess what's working and what isn't. Be willing to adjust your system as needed.

7. Celebrate Small Wins: Acknowledge your progress, whether it's unsubscribing from 10 newsletters or maintaining Inbox Zero for a week.

Taming your inbox is a crucial step in your journey towards digital minimalism. By implementing effective email management techniques, ruthlessly unsubscribing from unnecessary communications, and striving for Inbox Zero, you can transform your email from a source of stress to a tool that enhances your productivity and peace of mind.

Remember, the goal is not perfection, but improvement. Each step you take towards better email management is a step towards a more intentional and less cluttered digital life. As you implement these strategies, you may find that you're not just saving time and reducing stress, but also improving your communication skills and professional relationships.

In the next chapter, we'll explore how to apply minimalist principles to your social media use, another significant source of digital clutter for many people. By combining effective email management with mindful social media habits, you'll be well on your way to a more focused and intentional digital life.

Social Media Detox

In our increasingly connected world, social media has become an integral part of many people's daily lives. While these platforms offer benefits such as staying connected with friends and family, accessing information, and building professional networks, they can also be significant sources of distraction, anxiety, and digital clutter. This chapter will guide you through the process of assessing your social media usage, implementing techniques to reduce consumption, and cultivating more meaningful online connections.

Assessing Your Social Media Usage

Before embarking on a social media detox, it's crucial to understand your current usage patterns and the impact social media has on your life. This self-assessment will provide valuable insights and motivation for change.

1. Track Your Time

Start by accurately measuring how much time you spend on social media:

- Use built-in tools like Screen Time (iOS) or Digital Well being (Android)
  - Try third-party apps like Rescue Time or Moment for more detailed tracking
  - Keep a manual log for a week, noting when and why you use social media

2. Analyze Your Usage Patterns

Look for patterns in your social media use:

- What times of day do you use social media most?
  - Which apps do you use most frequently?
  - What triggers you to check social media? (e.g., boredom, stress, FOMO)

3. Reflect on the Impact

Consider how social media affects various aspects of your life:

- Productivity: Does it distract you from work or studies?
  - Mental health: How does it impact your mood, anxiety levels, or self-esteem?
  - Relationships: Does it enhance or detract from your real-world connections?
  - Sleep: Does nighttime usage affect your sleep quality?

4. Identify Your Goals

Based on your reflection, set clear goals for your social media usage:

- Do you want to reduce overall time spent?
  - Are there specific platforms you want to use less?
  - What positive aspects of social media do you want to maintain?

5. Conduct a Content Audit

Evaluate the content you consume on social media:

- Which accounts or types of content add value to your life?
  - Which ones tend to waste your time or negatively impact your mood?

- Are there any topics or types of content you want to see more or less of?

6. Assess Your Sharing Habits

Reflect on your own social media sharing behavior:

- How often do you post, and what motivates you to share?
  - Do you feel pressure to present a certain image online?
  - How does sharing affect your real-world experiences?

7. Consider Your Notification Settings

Review how often social media apps interrupt your day:

- How many notifications do you receive daily from each app?
  - Which notifications are truly important, and which are just noise?

By thoroughly assessing your social media usage, you'll gain a clearer picture of your habits and their impact on your life. This understanding will inform and motivate your efforts to create a healthier relationship with social media.

Techniques for Reducing Social Media Consumption

Now that you've assessed your social media usage, it's time to implement strategies to reduce consumption and reclaim your time and attention.

1. Set Clear Boundaries

Establish specific times for social media use:

- Designate "social media hours" and stick to them
  - Create social media-free zones (e.g., bedroom, dining table)
  - Implement a "no phone" rule during certain activities or times of day

2. Use Technology to Your Advantage

Leverage apps and settings to limit your access:

- Use app blockers like Freedom or App Block to restrict access during certain hours
    - Set daily time limits for social media apps using built-in phone features
    - Use browser extensions like StayFocusd to limit time on social media websites

3. Curate Your Feed

Make your social media experiences more intentional:

- Follow or mute accounts that don't add value to your life
    - Use lists or groups to organize content and control what you see
    - Follow accounts that align with your goals and interests

4. Disable Push Notifications

Reduce the temptation to constantly check your phone:

- Turn off push notifications for all social media apps
    - If necessary, allow notifications only from select individuals

5. Practice Mindful Usage

When you do use social media, do so with intention:

- Before opening an app, pause and ask yourself why you're doing it
    - Set a specific goal or time limit for each session
    - Be an active, engaged user rather than a passive stroller

6. Find Alternative Activities

Replace mindless scrolling with more fulfilling activities:

- Keep a list of alternative activities (e.g., reading, exercise, hobbies)
    - When tempted to check social media, choose an activity from your list instead

7. Implement Regular Digital Detoxes

Take periodic breaks from social media:

- Try a weekend without social media
    - Participate in initiatives like "Digital Sabbath" (one day a week offline)
    - Consider a longer detox (e.g., a month-long social media fast)

8. Rearrange Your Phone

Make social media less accessible on your devices:

- Move social media apps off your home screen
    - Place them in a folder on a secondary screen
    - Consider deleting apps and accessing via browser instead

9. Practice the 'One In, One Out' Rule

For every new account you follow:

- Follow or mute an existing one
    - This helps maintain a manageable, valuable feed

10. Use Social Media with Purpose

Transform your usage from passive consumption to active engagement:

- Set specific goals for your social media use (e.g., professional networking, staying in touch with distant friends)
    - Limit your use to these purposeful activities

11. Create Physical Distance

Make it physically harder to access your devices:

- Keep your phone in another room while working
    - Use a locked container for your devices during certain hours

12. Educate Yourself on Platform Design

Understanding how social media platforms are designed to be addictive can help you resist their pull:

- Read books like "Hooked" by Nir Eyal or "Irresistible" by Adam Alter
    - Watch documentaries like "The Social Dilemma"

13. Use Gray scale Mode

Make your phone less visually appealing:

- Enable gray scale mode on your device
    - This can make scrolling through social media less enticing

14. Practice Delayed Gratification

When you feel the urge to check social media:

- Set a timer for 10 minutes

- If you still want to check after the timer goes off, allow yourself a brief session

15. Log Out After Each Use

Make accessing social media a conscious decision:

- Log out of social media apps after each use
  - The extra step of logging in can deter mindless checking

Remember, the goal isn't necessarily to eliminate social media entirely, but to create a healthier, more intentional relationship with these platforms. Be patient with yourself as you implement these changes, and don't be afraid to adjust your approach based on what works best for you.

Cultivating Meaningful Online Connections

While reducing social media consumption is important, it's equally crucial to ensure that the time you do spend online is meaningful and enriching. Here are strategies to cultivate more valuable online connections:

1. Quality Over Quantity

Focus on deepening connections rather than expanding your network:

- Regularly engage with a core group of friends or colleagues
  - Participate in meaningful discussions rather than surface-level interactions

2. Be Authentic

Present your genuine self online:

- Share real experiences and thoughts, not just highlights
    - Be honest about your challenges as well as your successes
    - Avoid the pressure to present a "perfect" life

3. Engage Actively

Move beyond passive scrolling:

- Comment thoughtfully on posts that resonate with you
    - Share content that you find genuinely valuable
    - Initiate conversations and ask questions

4. Use Private Messaging

Foster deeper connections through one-on-one communication:

- Use direct messages to have more personal conversations
    - Create small group chats for closer friends or colleagues

5. Join or Create Niche Communities

Find groups that align with your interests or goals:

- Participate in Facebook Groups or subreddits related to your hobbies or profession
    - Create your own group if you can't find an existing one that fits your needs

6. Schedule Virtual Meetups

Use social media to facilitate real-time interactions:

- Organize video calls with friends or family

- Participate in virtual events or webinars

7. Share Value

Focus on contributing positively to your online community:

- Share informative or inspiring content
    - Offer help or advice when appropriate
    - Celebrate others' achievements

8. Practice Active Listening

Even in online interactions, practice being fully present:

- Read posts and comments carefully before responding
    - Ask clarifying questions to ensure understanding
    - Acknowledge others' perspectives, even if you disagree

9. Set Interaction Goals

Approach social media with specific connection goals:

- Aim to have a meaningful interaction with one person each day
    - Try to learn something new from your network regularly

10. Use Social Media for Planning Real-World Meetups

Leverage online connections to enhance offline relationships:

- Use event features to organize get-together
    - Join local groups to find offline events in your area

11. Curate Your Network

Regularly assess and adjust your online connections:

- Follow accounts that don't contribute positively to your life
  - Seek out and connect with individuals who inspire or challenge you

12. Practice Empathy and Kindness

Contribute to a more positive online environment:

- Respond to others with kindness and understanding
  - Avoid engaging in or encouraging negative behavior like trolling or cyberbullying

13. Share Your Expertise

Use your knowledge to add value to your network:

- Share insights from your professional or personal experiences
  - Offer thoughtful advice when asked

14. Engage in Collaborative Projects

Use social media to connect with others on shared goals:

- Participate in online challenges or group projects
  - Collaborate on creative or professional endeavors

15. Prioritize Privacy

Maintain healthy boundaries in your online interactions:

- Regularly review and adjust your privacy settings
  - Be mindful of what personal information you share online

16. Practice Gratitude

Express appreciation for your online connections:

- Thank people for sharing valuable content
  - Acknowledge how online friendships have positively impacted your life

17. Use Multimedia to Enhance Connections

Leverage various forms of content to connect more deeply:

- Share voice messages for a more personal touch
  - Use video content to convey emotions more effectively

18. Seek Diverse Perspectives

Use social media to broaden your horizons:

- Follow accounts that offer different viewpoints
  - Engage in respectful dialogues with people from diverse backgrounds

19. Support Others

Use your online presence to lift others up:

- Share and promote others' work or achievements
  - Offer encouragement and support during challenging times

20. Reflect on Your Interactions

Regularly assess the quality of your online connections:

- Consider which interactions leave you feeling energized or inspired

- Reflect on how you can contribute more meaningfully to your online community

By focusing on these strategies, you can transform your social media experience from one of passive consumption to active, meaningful engagement. Remember, the goal is to use these platforms as tools for genuine connection and personal growth, rather than sources of distraction or comparison.

A social media detox doesn't mean completely eliminating these platforms from your life. Instead, it's about creating a more intentional, balanced approach to social media use. By assessing your current habits, implementing strategies to reduce consumption, and focusing on cultivating meaningful online connections, you can transform your relationship with social media.

This process may take time and will likely involve some trial and error. Be patient with yourself and remember that small, consistent changes can lead to significant improvements in your digital well-being. As you progress in your social media detox, you may find that you're not only reclaiming your time and attention but also experiencing improved mental health, increased productivity, and more authentic connections both online and offline.

In the next chapter, we'll explore how to apply minimalist principles to your digital content consumption, helping you curate a more intentional and enriching online experience beyond social media.

Digital Content Consumption

In today's digital landscape, we're constantly bombarded with an overwhelming amount of content. From news articles and blog posts to streaming services and podcasts, the sheer volume of available information can be both a blessing and a curse. While having access to diverse content can broaden our horizons, it can also lead to information overload, decreased attention spans, and a sense of being constantly "plugged in." This chapter will guide you through the process of curating your digital content consumption to create a more balanced, intentional, and enriching information diet.

Curating Your News and Information Sources

In an era of "fake news," echo chambers, and information overload, curating reliable and diverse news sources is crucial. Here's how to create a more intentional news consumption habit:

1. Assess Your Current News Diet

Start by evaluating your existing news consumption habits:

- List all the news sources you regularly access
  - Note how often you check the news and through which mediums (e.g., websites, apps, social media)
  - Reflect on how your current news diet makes you feel (informed,

overwhelmed, anxious?)

2. Identify Your News Goals

Define what you want to achieve with your news consumption:

- Stay informed about specific topics or areas of interest
    - Understand diverse perspectives on key issues
    - Reduce anxiety related to constant news checking

3. Choose Quality Over Quantity

Focus on a few high-quality news sources rather than consuming everything:

- Look for sources with a reputation for accuracy and balanced reporting
    - Consider subscribing to a reputable newspaper or magazine
    - Use fact-checking websites to verify the credibility of news sources

4. Diversify Your Sources

Avoid getting trapped in an echo chamber:

- Include sources from different political perspectives
    - Explore international news sources for a global view
    - Mix traditional media with new media formats like podcasts or newsletters

5. Use News Aggregators Wisely

Leverage tools that can help you efficiently access diverse news:

- Try apps like Clipboard or Apple News that curate content from various sources

- Use RSS readers to create a personalized news feed
- Be cautious of algorithm-driven news feeds that may reinforce existing biases

6. Set News Consumption Boundaries

Create a structured approach to news consumption:

- Designate specific times for checking news (e.g., morning and evening)
  - Avoid constantly refreshing news sites or apps throughout the day
  - Consider a "news fast" one day a week to reduce information overload

7. Practice Slow News Consumption

Shift from constant updates to more in-depth, thoughtful consumption:

- Focus on long-form articles that provide context and analysis
  - Read weekly or monthly publications for a more measured perspective
  - Take time to reflect on and discuss news items rather than just consuming them

8. Develop Media Literacy Skills

Enhance your ability to critically evaluate news and information:

- Learn to distinguish between facts, opinions, and speculation in reporting
  - Be aware of your own biases and how they might affect your interpretation of news
  - Look for primary sources when possible, rather than relying solely on commentary

9. Use Social Media for News Judiciously

If you use social media for news, do so mindfully:

- Follow official accounts of reputable news organizations
    - Be skeptical of sensational headlines and check sources before sharing
    - Use lists or groups to curate a focused news feed within social platforms

10. Consider Paid Subscriptions

Support quality journalism and gain access to more in-depth content:

- Choose one or two paid subscriptions that align with your interests and values
    - Take advantage of free trials to test different publications before committing

By implementing these strategies, you can create a more intentional and balanced news consumption habit. Remember, the goal is to stay informed without becoming overwhelmed or overly anxious about current events.

Managing Subscriptions and Streaming Services

The proliferation of subscription-based services and streaming platforms has revolutionized how we consume content. However, it's easy to accumulate more subscriptions than we can realistically use. Here's how to manage your digital subscriptions more effectively:

1. Conduct a Subscription Audit

Start by taking stock of all your current subscriptions:

- List all digital subscriptions (e.g., streaming services, news sites, apps)
    - Note the monthly cost of each subscription
    - Calculate the total amount you're spending on subscriptions monthly and

annually

2. Assess Usage and Value

For each subscription, consider:

- How often do you actually use it?
    - Does it provide unique content you can't get elsewhere?
    - Does the value you receive justify the cost?

3. Implement the "One In, One Out" Rule

To prevent subscription creep:

- For every new subscription you add, cancel an existing one
    - This helps maintain a manageable number of subscriptions

4. Rotate Subscriptions

Instead of maintaining multiple subscriptions year-round:

- Keep one or two core subscriptions that you use regularly
    - Rotate other subscriptions based on specific content you want to access
    - Take advantage of free trials, but set reminders to cancel if you don't want to continue

5. Share Subscriptions When Possible

Many services allow multiple users or family sharing:

- Set up family plans for services you use frequently
    - Consider sharing costs with friends or family for services that allow it
    - Be aware of and respect the terms of service for each platform

6. Use Free Alternatives

Explore free options before committing to paid subscriptions:

- Use library apps like Libby for e-books and audio books
  - Check out free streaming platforms like Pluto TV or Tubi
  - Look for free versions of paid apps that might meet your needs

7. Set a Subscription Budget

Allocate a specific amount for digital subscriptions:

- Decide on a monthly budget for all your digital subscriptions
  - Prioritize which subscriptions fit within this budget
  - Regularly review and adjust your budget as needed

8. Manage Auto-Renewals

Take control of your subscription renewals:

- Turn off auto-renewal for subscriptions you're unsure about
  - Set calendar reminders to review subscriptions before they renew
  - Consider using a service like Truebill to help manage and cancel subscriptions

9. Batch Your Content Consumption

Make the most of your subscriptions by batching your viewing or reading:

- Designate specific times for using subscription services
  - Consider "binge months" where you catch up on content from a specific service, then cancel

10. Regularly Reassess Your Needs

Your content needs and interests may change over time:

- Conduct a subscription review every 3-6 months
    - Be willing to let go of subscriptions that no longer serve you
    - Stay open to new services that might better meet your current needs

By managing your subscriptions more intentionally, you can reduce digital clutter, save money, and ensure that the content you're paying for aligns with your values and interests.

Developing Healthy Reading and Viewing Habits

With an endless stream of content at our fingertips, it's crucial to develop healthy habits for consuming digital media. Here are strategies to make your reading and viewing more intentional and enriching:

1. Set Clear Intentions

Before engaging with digital content, ask yourself:

- What do I hope to gain from this content?
    - Is this the best use of my time right now?
    - How does this align with my goals and values?

2. Practice Mindful Consumption

Engage with content more consciously:

- Give your full attention to what you're reading or watching
    - Avoid multitasking or having multiple tabs open
    - Take breaks to reflect on and process the content

3. Implement the 20-20-20 Rule

To reduce digital eye strain:

- Every 20 minutes, take a 20-second break
    - Look at something 20 feet away
    - This helps reduce eye fatigue and improves focus

4. Create a Digital Reading List

Instead of immediately consuming every interesting piece of content you find:

- Use a "read it later" app like Pocket or Instapaper
    - Regularly review and curate your reading list
    - Set aside specific times for working through your saved content

5. Embrace Slow Reading

Counteract the tendency to skim or speed-read everything:

- Choose one or two articles a week for deep, careful reading
    - Take notes or highlight key points
    - Reflect on or discuss the content after reading

6. Practice Active Viewing

When watching videos or streaming content:

- Choose content intentionally rather than passively browsing
    - Take short breaks between episodes to reflect on what you've watched
    - Engage in discussions about the content with others

7. Set Content Consumption Limits

Establish boundaries around your digital media consumption:

- Use app timers to limit time spent on reading or streaming apps
    - Designate certain hours of the day as "content-free" time
    - Try a "digital sunset" by avoiding screens for an hour before bed

8. Balance Digital and Physical Media

Incorporate non-digital content into your routine:

- Read physical books or magazines
    - Listen to podcasts while doing other activities
    - Attend live events or performances when possible

9. Curate Your Content Environment

Create spaces conducive to focused reading or viewing:

- Designate a comfortable, distraction-free area for reading
    - Use browser extensions to minimize distractions on reading websites
    - Create a cozy, dedicated space for intentional TV or movie watching

10. Practice Content Fasting

Regularly take breaks from content consumption:

- Try a 24-hour period without consuming any digital content
    - Use this time for reflection, creativity, or real-world experiences
    - Notice how you feel during and after these fasts

11. Engage in Active Learning

Transform passive consumption into active learning:

- Take notes on important content you consume
    - Try to teach or explain key concepts to someone else
    - Look for ways to apply what you've learned in your daily life

12. Cultivate a Growth Mindset

Approach your content consumption with curiosity and openness:

- Seek out content that challenges your existing beliefs
    - Engage with difficult or complex material to stretch your understanding
    - Reflect on how your perspectives change over time

13. Practice Digital Nutrition

Think of your content consumption like your diet:

- Aim for a balanced "information diet" with a mix of educational, entertaining, and inspiring content
    - Be mindful of "empty calorie" content that doesn't provide real value
    - Regularly "detox" from low-quality or negative content

14. Use Technology to Support Healthy Habits

Leverage apps and tools designed to promote better digital habits:

- Try apps like Forest or Freedom to block distracting sites during reading time
    - Use e-readers with e-ink displays for a more eye-friendly reading experience
    - Explore apps that gamify or track your reading progress for motivation

15. Develop a Content Consumption Routine

Create structure around your digital media consumption:

- Designate specific times of day for different types of content (e.g., news in the morning, entertainment in the evening)
    - Create rituals around your consumption (e.g., a cup of tea with your evening reading)
    - Use transitions to mindfully start and end your content consumption sessions

16. Practice Gratitude and Reflection

Regularly reflect on the content you consume:

- Keep a journal of key insights or ideas from your reading and viewing
    - Practice gratitude for the access you have to diverse content
    - Reflect on how your content consumption habits are impacting your life and mindset

17. Engage in Content Creation

Balance consumption with creation:

- Write reviews or reflections on books you've read or shows you've watched
    - Create your own content (blog posts, videos, podcasts) inspired by what you've consumed
    - Participate in online discussions or book clubs to share your thoughts

18. Prioritize Quality Sleep

Recognize the impact of content consumption on your sleep:

- Avoid screens for at least an hour before bedtime
  - Use blue light filters on devices if you must use them in the evening
  - Choose calming, non-stimulating content for evening consumption

19. Be Mindful of Emotional Impact

Pay attention to how different types of content affect your mood and mental state:

- Notice which content leaves you feeling energized, inspired, or peaceful
  - Be aware of content that tends to increase anxiety, anger, or negative thinking
  - Adjust your consumption habits based on these observations

20. Celebrate Progress, Not Perfection

Remember that developing healthy digital consumption habits is a journey:

- Celebrate small improvements in your habits
  - Be patient with yourself if you slip into old patterns
  - Regularly reassess and adjust your strategies as needed

By implementing these strategies, you can transform your digital content consumption from a passive, often overwhelming experience into an intentional, enriching part of your life. Remember, the goal is not to eliminate digital content, but to create a healthier, more balanced relationship with the vast array of information and entertainment available to us in the digital age.

Conclusion

In our information-rich world, learning to curate our digital content consumption is a crucial skill. By thoughtfully selecting our news sources, managing our subscriptions, and developing healthy reading and viewing habits, we can create a digital diet that informs, entertains, and enriches our lives without overwhelming us.

As you implement these strategies, remember that everyone's ideal content consumption pattern will be different. The key is to find an approach that aligns with your values, supports your goals, and enhances your well-being. Be patient with yourself as you experiment with different techniques, and don't be afraid to adjust your approach as your needs and circumstances change.

In the next chapter, we'll explore how to leverage digital tools for productivity while maintaining a minimalist approach to technology use.

Digital Tools for Minimalism

I n our quest for digital minimalism, it may seem paradoxical to turn to more digital tools. However, when chosen carefully and used intentionally, certain digital tools can be powerful allies in our journey towards a more focused, simplified digital life. This chapter will explore a range of tools designed to enhance productivity, promote digital detox, and simplify digital security. By leveraging these tools, we can create a digital environment that supports our minimalist goals rather than detracting from them.

Productivity Apps That Promote Focus

In a world full of digital distractions, apps that help us maintain focus are invaluable. Here are some categories of productivity apps that can support your digital minimalism journey, along with specific examples:

1. Pomodoro Technique Apps

The Pomodoro Technique involves working in focused 25-minute intervals followed by short breaks. Apps that support this method include:

- Forest: Gamifies the Pomodoro Technique by growing virtual trees during focus sessions.
    - Focus To-Do: Combines Pomodoro timer with task management.
    - Be Focused: A simple, customization Pomodoro timer for Apple devices.

2. Distraction Blockers

These apps help eliminate digital distractions by blocking certain websites or apps:

- Freedom: Blocks distracting websites and apps across all your devices.
    - Cold Turkey: Allows for scheduling of distraction-free time periods.
    - Focus: A website blocker with customization blocking schedules.

3. Minimalist Writing Tools

For distraction-free writing, consider these streamlined apps:

- iA Writer: A clean, simple interface for focused writing.
    - Typora: A minimalist Markdown editor.
    - Hemingway Editor: Helps simplify and clarify your writing.

4. Task Management Apps

Stay organized with these streamlined task management tools:

- Todoist: A clean, intuitive to-do list app with cross-platform support.
    - Things: A beautifully designed task manager for Apple devices.
    - Microsoft To Do: A simple, effective task manager integrated with Microsoft 365.

5. Note-Taking Apps

Capture and organize your thoughts with these minimalist note-taking apps:

- Notion: A versatile workspace for notes, tasks, and collaboration.
    - Bear: A beautiful, flexible writing app for Apple devices.
    - Simple Note: A clean, simple note-taking app with cross-platform sync.

6. Time Tracking Apps

Understand how you spend your digital time with these trackers:

- Rescue Time: Automatically tracks time spent on applications and websites.
    - Toggl: A simple, user-friendly time tracker for projects and tasks.
    - Clockify: A free time tracker with detailed reporting features.

7. Focus Music Apps

These apps provide background sounds to enhance focus:

- Brain.fm: Offers AI-generated music designed to enhance focus.
    - Noisli: Allows you to mix different environmental sounds for a personalized ambiance.
    - Endel: Creates personalized soundscapes based on your circadian rhythm.

8. Habit-Forming Apps

Build positive digital habits with these tools:

- Habitica: Gamifies habit-forming by turning your goals into a role-playing game.
    - Streaks: A simple, visually appealing habit tracker for Apple devices.
    - Loop Habit Tracker: A minimalist, open-source habit tracker for Android.

When choosing productivity apps, consider the following:

- Simplicity: Opt for apps with clean, intuitive interfaces that won't add to your digital clutter.
    - Cross-platform availability: If you use multiple devices, choose apps that sync across platforms.
    - Export options: Ensure you can easily export your data if you decide to

switch apps.

   - Privacy: Review the app's privacy policy to understand how your data is used and protected.

Remember, the goal is to use these tools to enhance your productivity and focus, not to become dependent on them. Regularly assess whether each app is truly serving your digital minimalism goals.

Digital Detox and Screen Time Tracking Tools

As we strive for digital minimalism, it's crucial to be aware of our screen time and take regular breaks from our devices. Here are some tools to help you track and manage your digital consumption:

1. Built-in Screen Time Trackers

Most modern smartphones come with built-in screen time tracking:

- Screen Time (iOS): Provides detailed reports on device usage and allows setting app limits.

   - Digital Well being (Android): Offers similar features to Screen Time, including app timers and focus mode.

2. Third-Party Screen Time Trackers

For more detailed analytics or cross-platform tracking, consider:

- Rescue Time: Provides in-depth analysis of your digital activities across devices.

   - Moment: Tracks screen time and helps you set goals for reducing it.

   - Action Dash: A feature-rich digital well being app for Android.

3. App Blockers with Scheduling

These tools allow you to schedule device-free time:

- Freedom: Blocks apps and websites across all your devices on a set schedule.
  - App Block: Allows you to create profiles for different blocking scenarios.
  - Flipd: Locks your phone for set periods to encourage offline time.

4. Digital Detox Apps

These apps are specifically designed to help you disconnect:

- Off time: Blocks distracting apps and filters communication.
  - Space: Helps you set goals for phone usage and breaks them down into achievable targets.
  - Forest: Plants virtual trees while you're not using your phone, creating a visual representation of your offline time.

5. Mindfulness Apps

While not directly related to screen time, these apps can help you become more aware of your digital habits:

- Head space: Offers guided meditations, including some focused on technology use.
  - Calm: Provides meditation and mindfulness exercises to help reduce stress and improve focus.
  - Insight Timer: Offers a wide range of guided meditations, including some for digital mindfulness.

6. Browser Extensions

For managing screen time on your computer:

- StayFocusd: Restricts the amount of time you can spend on time-wasting websites.

- Pause: Stops mindless browsing by making you wait before accessing certain sites.
- News Feed Eradicator: Replaces social media news feeds with inspiring quotes.

7. E-Reader Apps

To encourage reading without distractions:

- Kindle: Offers a distraction-free reading experience with adjustable text and lighting.
  - Apple Books: A clean, simple interface for reading on Apple devices.
  - Moon+ Reader: A customization e-reader for Android with a focus mode.

When using digital detox and screen time tracking tools, keep these tips in mind:

- Start small: Begin with modest goals for reducing screen time and gradually increase them.
  - Use positive reinforcement: Choose apps that encourage and reward you for meeting your goals.
  - Combine with offline activities: Plan engaging offline activities to fill the time you're saving from reduced screen use.
  - Involve family and friends: Consider using apps that allow you to compare and share goals with others for added motivation.
  - Regular review: Periodically review your progress and adjust your goals as needed.

Remember, the ultimate goal of these tools is to help you become more aware of your digital habits and gradually reduce your dependence on devices. Use them as aids in your journey towards digital minimalism, not as another form of digital dependency.

Password Managers and Digital Security Simplification

In our efforts to simplify our digital lives, we shouldn't overlook the importance of digital security. Password managers can significantly simplify our online security while also enhancing it. Here's an overview of password managers and other tools for simplifying your digital security:

1. Password Managers

These tools securely store and generate complex passwords for all your accounts:

- Last Pass: A user-friendly option with both free and premium tiers.
    - 1 Password: Known for its strong security features and clean interface.
    - Bitwarden: An open-source option with a generous free tier.
    - Dashlane: Offers additional features like VPN and dark web monitoring.

Key features to look for in a password manager:

- Strong encryption: Ensure your data is protected with industry-standard encryption.
    - Two-factor authentication: Adds an extra layer of security to your password vault.
    - Cross-platform support: Access your passwords on all your devices.
    - Password generator: Creates strong, unique passwords for each account.
    - Secure sharing: Safely share passwords with family or team members.
    - Emergency access: Allows trusted contacts to access your vault in emergencies.

2. Two-Factor Authentication (2FA) Apps

These apps add an extra layer of security to your accounts:

- Google Authentication: A simple, widely-supported 2FA app.
  - Authy: Offers cloud backups of your 2FA tokens.
  - Microsoft Authentication: Integrates well with Microsoft accounts and offers additional features.

3. VPN Services

Virtual Private Networks (VPNs) enhance your online privacy and security:

- NordVPN: Known for its strong security features and large server network.
  - ExpressVPN: Offers fast speeds and user-friendly apps.
  - ProtonVPN: Provides a free tier with unlimited data.

4. Secure Messaging Apps

For private communications, consider these encrypted messaging apps:

- Signal: Offers end-to-end encryption for messages, calls, and video chats.
  - WhatsApp: Widely used and offers end-to-end encryption for messages.
  - Telegram: Features secure chats and self-destructing messages.

5. File Encryption Tools

Protect sensitive files on your device or in the cloud:

- VeraCrypt: A free, open-source disk encryption software.
  - Cryptomator: Encrypts cloud storage files before they leave your device.
  - BoxCryptor: Works with multiple cloud storage services to encrypt your files.

6. Security Audit Tools

These tools help you assess and improve your overall digital security:

- Have I Been Pwned: Checks if your email has been involved in known data breaches.
    - Security Planner: Provides personalized recommendations for improving your digital security.
    - Qualys SSL Labs: Tests the SSL/TLS configuration of websites you use.

7. Password-Less Authentication Tools

As we move towards simpler, more secure authentication methods:

- YubiKey: A hardware security key for two-factor authentication.
    - Windows Hello: Facial recognition and fingerprint login for Windows devices.
    - Apple's Face ID and Touch ID: Biometric authentication for Apple devices.

Tips for simplifying your digital security:

1. Use a password manager: This allows you to have strong, unique passwords for all accounts without having to remember them.

2. Enable two-factor authentication: Wherever possible, add this extra layer of security to your accounts.

3. Regularly update software: Keep all your devices and applications up-to-date to protect against known vulnerabilities.

4. Use biometric authentication: When available, use fingerprint or facial recognition for quicker, secure access to your devices.

5. Simplify your accounts: Close unused accounts to reduce your digital footprint and potential attack surface.

6. Use single sign-on (SSO) judiciously: While SSO can simplify your logins,

be cautious about which services you allow to access your main accounts.

7. Regularly review account access: Periodically check which apps and services have access to your main accounts (like Google or Facebook) and revoke unnecessary permissions.

8. Use secure, private browsing: Consider using a privacy-focused browser like Brave or DuckDuckGo's mobile browser.

9. Implement a VPN: Use a VPN service, especially when on public Wi-Fi networks.

10. Educate yourself: Stay informed about current digital security best practices and common threats.

Remember, the goal of these tools is to simplify and strengthen your digital security, not to add complexity to your digital life. Choose the tools that best fit your needs and gradually incorporate them into your digital routine.

The tools discussed in this chapter can be powerful allies in your journey towards digital minimalism. From apps that promote focus and productivity to those that help you manage screen time and simplify your digital security, these tools can help create a digital environment that aligns with your minimalist goals.

However, it's crucial to approach these tools with the same mindfulness we apply to other aspects of our digital lives. Regularly assess whether each tool is truly serving your needs and contributing to a simpler, more intentional digital lifestyle. Don't be afraid to experiment with different tools, but also be willing to let go of those that aren't providing significant value.

Remember, digital minimalism isn't about using the most cutting-edge tools or having the perfect app ecosystem. It's about creating a digital environment that supports your values, enhances your productivity, and allows you to focus on what truly matters in your life. Use these tools as aids in your journey, not as ends in themselves.

In the next chapter, we'll explore strategies for maintaining your digital minimalism practices over the long term, including how to adapt your approach as technology and your own needs evolve.

Creating a Sustainable Digital Routine

In our journey towards digital minimalism, one of the most crucial steps is establishing a sustainable digital routine. This involves thoughtfully integrating technology into our daily lives in a way that supports our goals and values without overwhelming us. In this chapter, we'll explore strategies for designing your ideal digital day, implementing regular breaks from technology, and striking a balance between online and offline activities.

Designing Your Ideal Digital Day

Creating an ideal digital day involves intentionally structuring your use of technology to maximize productivity, well-being, and personal fulfillment. Here's a step-by-step approach to designing your ideal digital day:

1. Start with Self-Reflection

Before diving into the specifics of your digital routine, take some time to reflect on your goals, values, and priorities. Ask yourself:

- What are my most important personal and professional goals?
    - How can technology help me achieve these goals?
    - What aspects of my current digital habits are hindering my progress?
    - When do I feel most productive and focused during the day?
    - What offline activities are essential for my well-being?

2. Map Out Your Ideal Day

Sketch out a rough timeline of your ideal day, including both digital and non-digital activities. Consider:

- Wake-up and bedtime routines
    - Work or study hours
    - Meal times
    - Exercise or physical activity
    - Social interactions
    - Leisure time
    - Personal development or hobby time

3. Identify Essential Digital Activities

List the digital activities that are truly necessary for your work, relationships, and personal growth. These might include:

- Checking and responding to important emails
    - Using specific software for work or study
    - Connecting with family and friends
    - Accessing important information or news
    - Engaging in online learning or skill development

4. Allocate Time for Digital Tasks

Assign specific time blocks for your essential digital activities. Consider:

- Batch processing emails at set times rather than constantly checking
    - Scheduling focused work sessions with minimal digital interruptions
    - Setting aside time for intentional social media use or online communication

5. Establish Digital-Free Zones and Times

Identify parts of your day that would benefit from being completely tech-free. For example:

- The first hour after waking up
    - During meals
    - The hour before bedtime
    - During exercise or outdoor activities
    - During face-to-face social interactions

6. Plan for Transitions

Create rituals or habits that help you transition between digital and non-digital activities. These might include:

- A short meditation or breathing exercise before opening your computer
    - A brief walk or stretch after a period of screen time
    - A cup of tea while reviewing your to-do list

7. Incorporate Mindful Tech Use

For the digital activities you do include, plan to engage with them mindfully. This could involve:

- Setting clear intentions before using social media or checking email
    - Using apps or browser extensions that promote focused work
    - Practicing gratitude for the benefits technology brings to your life

8. Allow for Flexibility

While structure is important, build some flexibility into your routine to account for unexpected events or changing needs.

9. Use Technology to Support Your Routine

Leverage digital tools that can help you maintain your ideal routine:

- Use calendar apps to schedule your day
    - Set reminders for digital-free times
    - Use apps that track your digital usage and help you stay accountable

10. Regular Review and Adjustment

Plan to review your digital routine regularly (e.g., weekly or monthly) and make adjustments as needed. What works for you may change over time, so be prepared to evolve your routine.

Example of an Ideal Digital Day:

- 6:00 AM: Wake up, avoid checking phone
    - 6:30 AM: 30-minute workout (tech-free)
    - 7:15 AM: Shower and breakfast (tech-free)
    - 8:00 AM: Check and respond to urgent emails (30 minutes)
    - 8:30 AM - 12:00 PM: Focused work with minimal digital interruptions
    - 12:00 PM: Lunch break (tech-free)
    - 1:00 PM - 3:00 PM: Meetings or collaborative work
    - 3:00 PM - 3:30 PM: Email and communication check
    - 3:30 PM - 5:30 PM: Focused work or learning time
    - 5:30 PM - 7:00 PM: Personal time (minimal tech use)
    - 7:00 PM - 9:00 PM: Family time (tech-free)
    - 9:00 PM - 10:00 PM: Relaxation (limited tech use, e.g., reading on e-reader)
    - 10:00 PM: Bedtime routine (tech-free)

Remember, this is just an example. Your ideal digital day should be tailored to your specific needs, responsibilities, and preferences.

Implementing Digital Sabbaths and Tech-Free Time Blocks

Regular breaks from technology are crucial for maintaining a healthy relationship with our digital tools. Here's how to implement digital sabbaths and tech-free time blocks into your routine:

Understanding Digital Sabbaths

A digital sabbath is an extended period, typically 24 hours, where you completely disconnect from digital technology. The benefits of this practice include:

- Reduced stress and anxiety
    - Improved sleep quality
    - Enhanced face-to-face relationships
    - Increased mindfulness and present-moment awareness
    - Boosted creativity and problem-solving skills

Implementing a Digital Sabbath

1. Choose Your Time: Select a 24-hour period that works best for your schedule. Many people choose Saturday evening to Sunday evening or Sunday morning to Monday morning.

2. Prepare in Advance: Inform friends, family, and colleagues that you'll be unreachable during this time. Set up auto-responders for email and voicemail if necessary.

3. Plan Offline Activities: Fill your digital sabbath with engaging offline activities like reading, outdoor exploration, creative projects, or quality time with loved ones.

4. Remove Temptations: Put your devices in a drawer or another room. If

possible, turn them off completely.

5. Use Physical Tools: Rely on physical tools like printed maps, physical books, or a traditional alarm clock during your digital sabbath.

6. Reflect on the Experience: After each digital sabbath, take some time to reflect on how it felt and what you learned about your relationship with technology.

Incorporating Tech-Free Time Blocks

In addition to a weekly digital sabbath, incorporating shorter tech-free time blocks throughout your week can be beneficial. Here are some strategies:

1. Morning Routine: Keep the first hour of your day tech-free. Use this time for meditation, journaling, exercise, or enjoying a leisurely breakfast.

2. Mealtime: Make all meals tech-free zones. Focus on the food and the company (if you're eating with others).

3. Work Breaks: Take short, tech-free breaks during your workday. A 10-15 minute walk without your phone can refresh your mind and boost productivity.

4. Evening Wind-Down: Implement a "digital sunset" by turning off screens 1-2 hours before bedtime. Use this time for relaxation, reading, or connecting with family.

5. Tech-Free Transitions: Create small tech-free buffers between activities. For example, take five deep breaths before checking your phone after a meeting.

6. Outdoor Time: Make any time spent in nature a tech-free experience. This

allows you to fully engage with your environment and reap the mental health benefits of nature.

7. Social Interactions: When meeting friends or family in person, agree to keep devices away. This promotes more meaningful, present conversations.

Overcoming Challenges

Implementing tech-free time can be challenging at first. Here are some tips for success:

- Start Small: If a full 24-hour sabbath seems daunting, start with shorter periods and gradually increase.
   - Use Physical Barriers: Put your phone in a locked drawer or use apps that restrict access during set times.
   - Find an Accountability Partner: Share your goals with a friend or family member who can support and encourage you.
   - Replace Digital Habits: For each digital habit you're trying to break, have a planned offline alternative.
   - Be Patient: It takes time to adjust to less screen time. Be kind to yourself and celebrate small victories.

Balancing Online and Offline Activities

Creating a sustainable digital routine isn't about completely eliminating technology from your life. Instead, it's about finding a healthy balance between your online and offline activities. Here are strategies to help you achieve this balance:

1. Audit Your Current Time Allocation

Before making changes, understand how you're currently spending your time:

- Use time-tracking apps to log your digital activities for a week
  - Note how much time you spend on offline activities
  - Reflect on whether this balance aligns with your values and goals

2. Set Clear Intentions for Online Time

When you do engage in online activities, do so with purpose:

- Before opening a device or app, pause and set an intention for what you want to accomplish
  - Use specific time limits for activities like social media browsing or online shopping
  - Focus on online activities that genuinely add value to your life

3. Prioritize High-Quality Offline Experiences

Invest time and energy in offline activities that enrich your life:

- Cultivate hobbies that don't require screens (e.g., gardening, painting, playing an instrument)
  - Prioritize face-to-face social interactions
  - Spend time in nature regularly
  - Engage in physical exercise or movement practices

4. Create a Balanced Daily Schedule

Design your day to include a mix of online and offline activities:

- Start your day with offline activities to set a positive tone
  - Intersperse offline breaks between periods of screen time
  - End your day with calming offline activities

5. Practice Mindful Transitions

Be intentional about how you switch between online and offline modes:

- Take a few deep breaths before switching on a device
    - Stretch or move your body after extended screen time
    - Use transition phrases like "I'm going offline now" to signal the end of digital engagement

6. Leverage Technology to Encourage Offline Activities

Use digital tools to support, not replace, offline experiences:

- Use fitness apps to track and motivate physical exercise
    - Try meditation apps to guide offline mindfulness practices
    - Use digital calendars to schedule and protect time for offline activities

7. Re frame Your Relationship with Technology

Shift your mindset to view technology as a tool, not a necessity:

- Regularly ask yourself, "Is this the best tool for this task?"
    - Challenge the notion that you need to be constantly connected
    - Appreciate the unique benefits of both online and offline experiences

8. Cultivate Offline Relationships

Prioritize and nurture your in-person relationships:

- Schedule regular face-to-face meetups with friends and family
    - Join local clubs or groups related to your interests
    - Volunteer in your community

9. Create Tech-Free Spaces in Your Home

Designate certain areas of your living space as tech-free zones:

- Keep bedrooms screen-free to improve sleep quality
    - Create a cozy reading nook without digital distractions
    - Make your dining area a no-phone zone to encourage mindful eating and
conversation

10. Practice Digital Minimalism in Your Online Activities

When you are online, apply minimalist principles:

- Regularly declutter your digital spaces (email, files, apps)
    - Follow or mute social media accounts that don't add value
    - Simplify your online subscriptions and notifications

11. Develop Offline Coping Mechanisms

Instead of turning to technology for comfort or distraction, develop offline
coping strategies:

- Practice deep breathing or progressive muscle relaxation for stress relief
    - Keep a physical journal for processing thoughts and emotions
    - Develop a list of go-to offline activities for when you're bored or anxious

12. Regularly Reassess and Adjust

Your ideal balance between online and offline activities may change over
time:

- Schedule monthly check-ins to reflect on your digital-offline balance
    - Be willing to adjust your routine as your needs and circumstances change
    - Celebrate progress and learn from challenges

Remember, the goal is not to completely eliminate technology from your life, but to use it in a way that enhances rather than detracts from your overall well-being. By thoughtfully designing your ideal digital day, implementing regular tech-free periods, and striving for a balance between online and offline activities, you can create a sustainable digital routine that supports a minimalist, intentional lifestyle.

This journey towards a balanced digital life is ongoing and personal. What works for one person may not work for another, so be patient with yourself as you experiment and find your own rhythm. The key is to remain mindful of how technology is impacting your life and to continuously strive for a balance that allows you to leverage the benefits of the digital world while also fully engaging with the richness of offline experiences.

Mindful Technology Use

In our digital age, technology has become an integral part of our daily lives. While it offers numerous benefits, it can also lead to mindless consumption and disconnection from our real-world experiences. This chapter explores how to cultivate a more mindful approach to technology use, developing intentional consumption habits, and leveraging technology to enhance rather than replace our real-life experiences.

Practicing Digital Mindfulness

Digital mindfulness involves bringing conscious awareness to our interactions with technology. By practicing digital mindfulness, we can use technology more intentionally and reduce its negative impacts on our well-being.

Understanding Digital Mindfulness

Digital mindfulness is rooted in the broader concept of mindfulness, which involves paying attention to the present moment without judgment. When applied to our digital lives, it means:

- Being aware of when, why, and how we use technology
  - Noticing the physical and emotional effects of our digital interactions
  - Making conscious choices about our technology use, rather than acting on autopilot

Strategies for Practicing Digital Mindfulness

1. Pause Before Engaging: Before reaching for your device, take a moment to ask yourself:
   - Why am I about to use this device?
   - Is this the best use of my time right now?
   - How do I feel, and will using technology improve or worsen my current state?

2. Set Intentions: Before each digital session, set a clear intention for what you want to accomplish. This could be as simple as "I'm going to check my email for 15 minutes" or "I'm going to research healthy dinner recipes."

3. Practice Mindful Browsing: When online, pay attention to your thoughts, feelings, and physical sensations. Notice when you feel the urge to click on another link or switch to a different app.

4. Use Mindful Notifications: Instead of reacting immediately to every notification, try using them as 'mindfulness bells.' When you hear a notification, take a deep breath and decide consciously whether to respond now or later.

5. Implement Mindful Transitions: Create a brief mindfulness practice for transitioning between digital and non-digital activities. For example, take three deep breaths before turning on your computer and after turning it off.

6. Practice Gratitude: Regularly reflect on the positive aspects of technology in your life. This can help foster a more balanced and appreciative relationship with your devices.

7. Body Awareness: Pay attention to your posture and physical sensations while using devices. Set reminders to do periodic body scans and adjust your position if needed.

8. Mindful Listening: When using technology for communication (e.g., video calls), practice active listening. Focus fully on the person speaking, rather than multitasking or getting distracted by your own thoughts.

9. Digital Detox Moments: Incorporate short "digital detox" moments throughout your day. These can be as brief as taking a few mindful breaths between checking emails.

10. Reflect on Digital Interactions: At the end of each day, take a few minutes to reflect on your digital interactions. Consider what felt meaningful and what felt draining.

Developing Intentional Consumption Habits

Intentional consumption involves making conscious choices about the digital content we engage with, rather than passively consuming whatever comes our way. Here are strategies to develop more intentional digital consumption habits:

1. Curate Your Digital Inputs

- Regularly audit your social media follows, email subscriptions, and news sources
    - Follow or unsubscribe from sources that don't add value to your life
    - Seek out high-quality, enriching content that aligns with your values and goals

2. Implement the 'Information Diet' Concept

- Treat digital content like food for your mind, and aim for a balanced, nutritious 'diet'
    - Limit 'junk' content that provides momentary entertainment but little lasting value

- Increase consumption of 'nourishing' content that educates, inspires, or promotes personal growth

3. Practice Slow Consumption

- Resist the urge to skim or multitask while consuming content
    - Choose one piece of content to focus on at a time
    - Take time to reflect on what you've read, watched, or listened to before moving on

4. Use the 'THINK' Framework Before Sharing

Before sharing content, ask yourself if it is:
    - True: Is the information accurate and from a reliable source?
    - Helpful: Will sharing this benefit others?
    - Inspiring: Does it motivate or uplift?
    - Necessary: Does it need to be said or shared?
    - Kind: Is it considerate and respectful?

5. Implement Waiting Periods

- When you feel the urge to buy something online, implement a 24-hour waiting period
    - For non-urgent emails or messages, wait an hour before responding
    - These waiting periods can help reduce impulsive behavior and promote more thoughtful engagement

6. Practice Digital Minimalism

- Regularly declutter your digital spaces (files, apps, bookmarks)
    - Keep only the digital tools and content that truly add value to your life
    - Simplify your digital workflows to reduce overwhelm and increase focus

7. Engage Actively, Not Passively

- Instead of mindless scrolling, engage actively with content
    - Take notes, write responses, or discuss what you've consumed with others
    - This active engagement helps deepen understanding and retention

8. Set Consumption Goals

- Define clear goals for your digital consumption (e.g., learning a new skill, staying informed about specific topics)
    - Regularly evaluate whether your consumption habits are helping you meet these goals

9. Use Technology to Support Intentional Consumption

- Leverage apps and browser extensions that promote focused reading or limit distractions
    - Use bookmarking tools to save content for later, intentional consumption
    - Utilize RSS feeds to curate your own 'information channel' rather than relying on algorithm-driven feeds

10. Practice Digital Sabbaths

- Designate regular periods (e.g., one day a week) for complete digital disconnection
    - Use this time to engage in offline activities and reflect on your digital consumption habits

Using Technology to Enhance, Not Replace, Real-Life Experiences

While technology offers many benefits, it's crucial to use it as a tool to enhance our real-world experiences rather than as a substitute for them. Here are strategies to ensure technology enriches rather than replaces real-life experiences:

1. Use Technology as a Bridge, Not a Barrier

- Leverage technology to connect with people in real life (e.g., planning meet-ups, finding local events)
   - Use social media to strengthen existing relationships, not as a replacement for face-to-face interaction
   - Be mindful of how technology use in social situations (e.g., checking phones during conversations) can create barriers

2. Enhance Experiences, Don't Just Capture Them

- While it's nice to document experiences, prioritize being present in the moment
   - Consider designating specific times for taking photos or videos, then putting devices away
   - Reflect on whether sharing experiences online enhances or detracts from your enjoyment of them

3. Use Technology to Facilitate Real-World Learning

- Leverage online resources to learn skills you can apply in the real world (e.g., cooking, DIY projects, language learning)
   - Use apps that encourage outdoor activities or exploration (e.g., hiking apps, geocaching)
   - Participate in online communities that organize real-world meetups or events

4. Practice Mindful Photography

- When taking photos, pause to really see and appreciate what you're capturing
   - Consider occasionally leaving your camera behind and experiencing

events without the pressure to document
  - Use photography as a tool for mindfulness, focusing on details you might otherwise miss

5. Leverage Technology for Mindfulness and Well-being

- Use meditation apps to guide offline mindfulness practices
  - Try apps that encourage regular breaks, stretching, or physical movement
  - Use technology to track and encourage healthy habits (e.g., sleep, exercise, water intake)

6. Enhance, Don't Replace, Human Interaction

- Use video calls to stay connected with distant loved ones, but prioritize in-person meetings when possible
  - In professional settings, consider when a face-to-face meeting might be more effective than digital communication
  - Be mindful of using technology as a crutch in social situations (e.g., looking at your phone when feeling uncomfortable)

7. Use Technology to Discover, Not Just Consume

- Use the internet to find new places to explore in your local area
  - Leverage travel apps to enhance your experiences in new places, not to view them solely through a screen
  - Use technology to learn about history or science in ways that complement real-world exploration

8. Balance Virtual and Physical Workspace

- While remote work offers many benefits, create opportunities for in-person collaboration when possible
  - Design your home office to promote well-being (e.g., proper ergonomics,

plants, natural light)

   - Use technology to enhance productivity, but incorporate offline tools and techniques as well

9. Mindful Gaming

- If you enjoy video games, look for ones that encourage physical movement or real-world skills

   - Consider how gaming can enhance social connections through multi-player or co-op experiences

   - Be mindful of the balance between virtual and real-world leisure activities

10. Technology-Enhanced Creativity

- Use digital tools to enhance creative hobbies, not replace hands-on creation

   - Explore how technology can open new avenues for creative expression

   - Share your creations online, but also find ways to showcase them in the physical world

11. Mindful Online Shopping

- Use online shopping as a tool for research, but consider the value of seeing and touching items in person

   - Support local businesses by using technology to find them, then visiting in person

   - Be mindful of how online shopping affects your relationship with material possessions

12. Digital-to-Physical Transitions

- Create rituals for transitioning from digital to physical activities (e.g., a short meditation after closing your laptop)

   - Use technology to set reminders for offline activities or real-world commitments

- Regularly reflect on how your use of technology is impacting your engagement with the physical world

By practicing digital mindfulness, developing intentional consumption habits, and using technology to enhance rather than replace real-life experiences, we can cultivate a healthier, more balanced relationship with our digital tools. Remember, the goal is not to eliminate technology from our lives, but to use it in ways that truly enrich our experiences and support our well-being.

As you implement these strategies, be patient with yourself and remember that developing mindful technology habits is an ongoing process. Regularly reflect on your progress, celebrate small victories, and be willing to adjust your approach as needed. With time and practice, you can create a digital life that enhances your real-world experiences and supports your overall well-being.

Digital Minimalism at Work

I n today's digital-first work environment, the principles of digital minimalism are more crucial than ever. Implementing these strategies can lead to increased productivity, reduced stress, and a better work-life balance. This chapter explores how to apply digital minimalism in the workplace, focusing on streamlining communication, managing distractions, and advocating for digital wellness in your organization.

Streamlining Digital Communication in the Workplace

Effective communication is crucial in any workplace, but the sheer volume of digital communication can often lead to overwhelm and decreased productivity. Here are strategies to streamline your digital communication at work:

1. Establish Clear Communication Channels

- Define specific platforms for different types of communication (e.g., email for formal requests, instant messaging for quick questions)
   - Create guidelines for when to use each channel to reduce confusion and overlap

2. Implement Email Management Techniques

- Use the "Two-Minute Rule": If an email can be responded to in two minutes

or less, do it immediately
  - Employ the "OHIO" principle: Only Handle It Once
  - Set up filters and folders to automatically sort incoming emails
  - Unsubscribe from unnecessary mailing lists and newsletters

3. Practice Batch Processing

- Check and respond to emails at set times during the day rather than constantly
  - Communicate your email checking schedule to colleagues to manage expectations

4. Use Asynchronous Communication When Possible

- Encourage the use of project management tools for updates and collaboration
  - Reduce the need for immediate responses by providing clear deadlines and expectations

5. Optimize Virtual Meetings

- Establish clear agendas and objectives for each meeting
  - Reduce the number and duration of meetings where possible
  - Consider if a meeting can be replaced by an email or shared document

6. Leverage Collaborative Tools Effectively

- Use shared documents for collaborative work to reduce back-and-forth emails
  - Utilize project management platforms to keep all project-related communication in one place

7. Implement a 'No Email' Day

- Designate one day a week (or month) as a 'No Email' day to encourage face-to-face or phone communication

8. Practice Mindful Communication

- Before sending a message, pause and consider if it's necessary and if the chosen medium is appropriate
    - Be concise and clear in your digital communications to reduce the need for clarifying exchanges

9. Use Templates and Canned Responses

- Create templates for frequently sent emails to save time and ensure consistency
    - Use canned responses for common queries

10. Encourage 'Deep Work' Periods

- Establish 'do not disturb' times for focused work, during which team members are not expected to respond to non-urgent communications

By implementing these strategies, you can significantly reduce the time and mental energy spent on digital communication, allowing for more focused and productive work time.

Managing Digital Distractions in a Professional Setting

Digital distractions can significantly impact productivity and job satisfaction. Here are strategies to manage these distractions effectively:

1. Conduct a Digital Distraction Audit

- Track your digital activities for a week to identify your main sources of distraction

- Note the times of day when you're most susceptible to distractions

2. Create a Distraction-Free Work Environment

- Close unnecessary browser tabs and applications
  - Use website blockers during focused work periods
  - Consider using a separate browser profile for work to keep personal browsing separate

3. Implement the Pomodoro Technique

- Work in focused 25-minute intervals followed by short breaks
  - Use this technique to stay focused and give yourself permission for controlled distraction during breaks

4. Customize Notification Settings

- Turn off non-essential notifications during work hours
  - Use 'Do Not Disturb' mode on your devices during focused work periods

5. Practice Digital Mindfulness

- Before checking your phone or opening a new tab, pause and ask yourself if it's necessary
  - Be aware of "infinity pools" (apps designed for endless scrolling) and set strict time limits for their use

6. Establish 'Tech Breaks'

- Schedule specific times for checking personal email, social media, or news
  - Having designated times can reduce the urge to constantly check these platforms

7. Use Technology to Combat Technology

- Employ apps that track and limit your usage of distracting websites and applications
    - Use focus apps that block distractions for set periods

8. Create Physical Barriers

- Keep your phone out of sight during focused work periods
    - If possible, designate a specific area for non-work related digital activities

9. Practice the 'One-Tab' Rule

- When working on a task, keep only the necessary tab or application open
    - This reduces the temptation to switch between tasks

10. Develop a Startup and Shutdown Ritual

- Begin each workday by reviewing your tasks and setting intentions
    - End each day by clearing your digital workspace and planning for the next day

11. Leverage 'Micro-Boundaries'

- Take short breaks between tasks to reset your focus
    - Use these breaks to stretch, practice deep breathing, or do a quick mindfulness exercise

12. Educate Yourself on the Impacts of Multitasking

- Understand the cognitive costs of constant task-switching
    - Share this knowledge with colleagues to create a culture that values focused work

By implementing these strategies, you can create a work environment that promotes focus and reduces the negative impacts of digital distractions.

Advocating for Digital Wellness in Your Organization

Creating a culture of digital wellness in your workplace can lead to improved productivity, job satisfaction, and overall well-being for all employees. Here are strategies for advocating digital wellness in your organization:

1. Lead by Example

- Implement digital minimalism practices in your own work routine
    - Share your experiences and the benefits you've observed with colleagues and superiors

2. Educate Your Team

- Organize workshops or lunch-and-learn sessions on digital wellness
    - Share articles, books, or podcasts about digital minimalism with your team

3. Propose a Digital Wellness Policy

- Draft a proposal for a company-wide digital wellness policy
    - Include guidelines for email use, meeting schedules, and expectations for after-hours communication

4. Encourage 'Offline' Time

- Propose device-free meetings or brainstorming sessions
    - Suggest 'walking meetings' for one-on-one discussions

5. Promote Work-Life Balance

- Advocate for clear boundaries between work and personal time
  - Encourage the use of vacation time and 'digital detox' days

6. Implement 'Focus Time' in Team Schedules

- Propose designated periods for uninterrupted, focused work
  - Encourage team members to respect these focus times by avoiding non-urgent communications

7. Suggest Digital Wellness Challenges

- Organize team or company-wide challenges related to digital wellness (e.g., a 'no email after 6 pm' week)
  - Offer incentives for participation and goal achievement

8. Advocate for Mindful Technology Use

- Suggest guidelines for mindful use of technology in meetings (e.g., laptops closed unless necessary)
  - Propose a 'no phones at lunch' policy to encourage face-to-face interaction

9. Promote Digital Literacy

- Organize training sessions on effective use of digital tools
  - Encourage efficient use of technology to reduce unnecessary digital clutter

10. Create a Digital Wellness Committee

- Propose the formation of a committee dedicated to promoting digital wellness in the workplace
  - Include representatives from different departments to ensure diverse perspectives

11. Conduct Regular Digital Wellness Assessments

- Suggest periodic surveys to assess the digital well-being of employees
  - Use the results to inform and adjust digital wellness initiatives

12. Advocate for Ergonomic and Wellness-Focused Workspace

- Propose standing desks, ergonomic chairs, or other equipment that promotes physical well-being during computer use
  - Suggest the creation of 'tech-free' zones in the office for breaks and informal meetings

13. Encourage Peer Support

- Start a digital wellness support group where colleagues can share tips and challenges
  - Implement a buddy system for accountability in digital minimalism practices

14. Propose Digital Wellness as Part of Employee Benefits

- Advocate for including digital wellness resources (e.g., subscriptions to mindfulness apps) as part of employee benefits
  - Suggest offering 'digital detox' days as part of personal time off

15. Integrate Digital Wellness into Performance Reviews

- Propose including digital wellness practices as part of performance evaluations
  - Emphasize the importance of quality work over quantity of hours spent online

16. Celebrate Digital Wellness Successes

- Recognize and celebrate individuals or teams who successfully implement digital wellness practices
  - Share success stories to inspire others in the organization

17. Address Potential Resistance

- Anticipate concerns about reduced connectivity or responsiveness
  - Prepare data and case studies that demonstrate the benefits of digital wellness in the workplace

18. Collaborate with HR and IT Departments

- Work with Human Resources to integrate digital wellness into company culture and policies
  - Collaborate with IT to implement tools and systems that support digital minimalism

19. Propose a Digital Mentor Program

- Suggest a program where digitally mindful employees can mentor others in implementing these practices

20. Advocate for Continuous Improvement

- Encourage regular review and adjustment of digital wellness initiatives
  - Stay informed about new research and best practices in digital wellness and share these with your organization

Implementing digital minimalism in the workplace is an ongoing process that requires patience, persistence, and collaboration. As you advocate for these changes, remember that small, consistent steps can lead to significant improvements over time. Here are some final thoughts to consider:

- Be Patient: Organizational change takes time. Be prepared for gradual adoption and celebrate small victories along the way.

- Stay Flexible: Be open to adapting your strategies based on feedback and results. What works for one team or individual may not work for another.

- Emphasize Benefits: When advocating for digital wellness, focus on the benefits to both employees and the organization, such as increased productivity, improved job satisfaction, and reduced burnout.

- Address Concerns: Be prepared to address concerns about reduced connectivity or responsiveness. Emphasize that the goal is more effective, not less, communication and work.

- Continuous Learning: Stay informed about new research and best practices in digital wellness and workplace productivity. Share your learning with your organization.

- Personal Practice: Continue to refine your own digital minimalism practices. Your personal experience will be your most powerful tool in advocating for change.

Remember, the goal of digital minimalism at work is not to eliminate technology, but to use it more intentionally and effectively. By streamlining digital communication, managing distractions, and advocating for digital wellness, you can help create a work environment that promotes focus, productivity, and well-being in the digital age.

As you implement these strategies, be prepared for challenges and setbacks. Change can be uncomfortable, and some colleagues may be resistant at first. Stay committed to your vision of a more digitally mindful workplace, and let the positive results speak for themselves. Over time, you may find that your efforts not only improve your own work experience but also contribute to a more positive and productive work culture for everyone in your organization.

Teaching Digital Minimalism to Others

As you embrace digital minimalism in your own life, you may find yourself wanting to share these principles with others. Whether you're a parent concerned about your children's screen time, a friend noticing the toll of constant connectivity on your social circle, or an individual looking to build a community of like-minded digital minimalists, this chapter will provide strategies for effectively teaching and promoting digital minimalism to others.

Guiding Children and Teens Towards Healthy Tech Habits

In today's digital world, helping young people develop healthy relationships with technology is crucial. Here are strategies for guiding children and teens towards digital minimalism:

1. Lead by Example

Children often model their behavior after adults. Demonstrate healthy tech habits in your own life:

- Put your phone away during meals and family time
    - Engage in offline activities regularly
    - Talk about your own efforts to use technology mindfully

2. Establish Clear Guidelines

Create age-appropriate rules for technology use:

- Set screen time limits
    - Designate tech-free zones (e.g., bedrooms) and times (e.g., during meals)
    - Establish consequences for breaking these rules, and be consistent in enforcing them

3. Educate About Digital Citizenship

Teach children about responsible online behavior:

- Discuss online privacy and the permanence of digital actions
    - Teach critical thinking skills for evaluating online information
    - Address cyberbullying and the importance of kindness online

4. Encourage Offline Interests

Help children develop hobbies and interests that don't involve screens:

- Introduce them to sports, arts, or outdoor activities
    - Encourage reading physical books
    - Plan regular family outings to nature or cultural events

5. Use Technology Purposefully

When children do use technology, guide them towards purposeful use:

- Help them find educational apps and websites
    - Teach them to use technology as a tool for creation, not just consumption
    - Show them how to use productivity apps to manage schoolwork

6. Implement Gradual Changes

If current tech habits are unhealthy, make changes gradually:

- Start with small adjustments to avoid overwhelming resistance
    - Involve children in the process of creating new tech rules
    - Celebrate small victories and improvements

7. Teach Mindfulness

Introduce age-appropriate mindfulness techniques:

- Practice simple breathing exercises together
    - Encourage periodic "mindful moments" throughout the day
    - Discuss how they feel during and after extended screen time

8. Use Parental Controls Wisely

Leverage parental control features on devices:

- Set up content filters to protect against inappropriate material
    - Use screen time tracking tools to monitor usage
    - Gradually reduce restrictions as children demonstrate responsible use

9. Foster Open Communication

Create an environment where children feel comfortable discussing their digital lives:

- Ask open-ended questions about their online experiences
    - Listen without judgment and offer guidance when needed
    - Share your own digital challenges and how you overcome them

10. Emphasize Balance

Help children understand the importance of a balanced life:

- Discuss the benefits of both online and offline activities
    - Help them create schedules that include a mix of screen and non-screen time
    - Encourage self-reflection on how different activities make them feel

11. Address FOMO (Fear of Missing Out)

Help teens navigate social pressures related to constant connectivity:

- Discuss the reality behind curated social media posts
    - Encourage real-world social connections
    - Teach strategies for managing FOMO, like practicing gratitude

12. Provide Alternatives to Smartphones

For younger children and preteens, consider alternatives to full-featured smartphones:

- Use basic phones that only allow calls and texts
    - Explore smartwatches designed for children with limited features
    - Gradually introduce more advanced devices as they demonstrate readiness

13. Teach Digital Literacy

Help children become savvy digital consumers:

- Show them how to fact-check information
    - Discuss advertising strategies and how to identify sponsored content
    - Teach them about algorithms and how they shape online experiences

14. Make It Fun

Turn digital minimalism into an engaging challenge:

- Create family challenges, like a "no-screen Saturday"
    - Use gamification to encourage healthy tech habits
    - Reward progress with special family activities or privileges

Remember, guiding children and teens towards digital minimalism is an ongoing process that requires patience, consistency, and adaptability. As they grow and technology evolves, be prepared to adjust your approach while maintaining the core principles of intentional and balanced technology use.

Influencing Friends and Family

Sharing digital minimalism principles with adult friends and family requires a different approach. Here are strategies for influencing your peers:

1. Share Your Personal Experience

Be open about your own journey with digital minimalism:

- Discuss the challenges you've faced and overcome
    - Share the benefits you've experienced, both personal and professional
    - Be honest about ongoing struggles to present a realistic picture

2. Lead by Example

Demonstrate digital minimalism in your interactions:

- Be fully present during in-person conversations
    - Respond to messages at designated times rather than immediately
    - Share how you're spending your offline time in positive ways

3. Offer Gentle Suggestions

Instead of criticizing others' habits, offer positive alternatives:

- Suggest offline activities for get-together
  - Share interesting articles or books about digital wellness
  - Introduce apps or tools that promote mindful tech use

4. Create Tech-Free Social Experiences

Organize gatherings that naturally encourage disconnection:

- Host a device-free dinner party
  - Plan outdoor activities or nature trips
  - Arrange game nights or book clubs

5. Be Patient and Non-Judgmental

Recognize that everyone's journey is different:

- Avoid preaching or shaming others for their tech use
  - Offer support and encouragement for any steps towards digital minimalism
  - Be understanding of the challenges others may face in changing habits

6. Highlight the Benefits

Focus on the positive outcomes of digital minimalism:

- Share how it's improved your relationships
  - Discuss gains in productivity or creativity
  - Talk about improvements in mental health or stress levels

7. Address Common Concerns

Be prepared to discuss common objections to digital minimalism:

- Offer solutions for staying connected while reducing overall tech use
    - Discuss how to balance professional needs with digital wellness
    - Share strategies for overcoming FOMO

8. Use Analogies and Relatable Examples

Make digital minimalism concepts more accessible:

- Compare digital clutter to physical clutter in a home
    - Relate digital overwhelm to familiar experiences of stress or burnout
    - Use analogies from nutrition or fitness to explain digital "diet"

9. Offer Resources

Share helpful resources for those interested in learning more:

- Recommend books, podcasts, or documentaries on the topic
    - Share articles or blog posts about digital minimalism
    - Introduce apps or tools that support digital wellness

10. Respect Boundaries

Recognize when others aren't interested or ready:

- Don't push the topic if you sense resistance
    - Respect others' choices, even if they differ from yours
    - Be available for support if they decide to explore digital minimalism later

11. Collaborate on Challenges

Propose joint efforts to reduce digital clutter:

- Suggest a group digital detox weekend
    - Create a friendly competition for reducing screen time
    - Start a book club focused on digital wellness topics

12. Share Success Stories

Highlight real-life examples of digital minimalism's impact:

- Share stories of public figures who practice digital minimalism
    - Discuss case studies or research on the benefits of reduced screen time
    - Tell stories of friends or colleagues who've successfully adopted these practices

13. Offer Practical Tips

Provide actionable advice for getting started:

- Share your own "starter kit" of digital minimalism practices
    - Offer tips for common challenges, like reducing email overload
    - Suggest small, achievable steps for beginning the journey

14. Foster Ongoing Conversations

Keep the dialogue about digital habits open and ongoing:

- Check in with friends about their tech use and challenges
    - Share new insights or strategies you discover
    - Create a safe space for discussing digital wellness concerns

Remember, influencing friends and family is about planting seeds and nurturing interest, not forcing change. By living your own digital minimalist lifestyle and sharing its benefits, you can inspire others to explore this path for themselves.

Building a Community of Digital Minimalists

Creating a community can provide support, accountability, and shared learning experiences for those interested in digital minimalism. Here's how to build and nurture such a community:

1. Start Small

Begin with a core group of interested individuals:

- Reach out to friends or colleagues who've expressed interest in digital wellness
   - Create a small group chat or email list to share ideas and support
   - Start with a manageable size to ensure active participation

2. Define Your Community's Purpose

Clarify the goals and focus of your digital minimalist community:

- Is it primarily for support and accountability?
   - Will you focus on learning and sharing resources?
   - Do you want to organize offline activities or challenges?

3. Choose Communication Channels Wisely

Select platforms that align with digital minimalist principles:

- Consider using less addictive platforms like email groups or forums
   - If using social media, set clear guidelines for usage
   - Explore alternatives like Signal for private group chats

4. Establish Community Guidelines

Create a framework for respectful and productive interactions:

- Encourage supportive, non-judgmental communication
    - Set expectations for participation and sharing
    - Establish rules about privacy and confidentiality

5. Regular Check-Ins and Challenges

Keep the community engaged with consistent activities:

- Host weekly or monthly check-ins to discuss progress and challenges
    - Organize digital detox challenges or experiments
    - Create themed discussions on various aspects of digital minimalism

6. Share Resources and Learning Opportunities

Facilitate ongoing education within the community:

- Share relevant articles, books, or podcasts
    - Invite guest speakers or experts for Q&A sessions
    - Encourage members to share their own insights and experiences

7. Organize In-Person Meetups

Foster real-world connections within your digital minimalist community:

- Arrange regular meetups for local members
    - Plan activities that align with digital minimalism principles
    - Consider hosting workshops or discussion groups

8. Celebrate Successes

Acknowledge and celebrate members' achievements:

- Share success stories within the community
  - Recognize milestones in members' digital minimalism journeys
  - Create a system for peer recognition and support

9. Provide Accountability Partners

Facilitate one-on-one support within the community:

- Pair members for regular check-ins and support
  - Encourage partners to set and review goals together
  - Rotate partnerships to build connections across the community

10. Leverage Online Tools Mindfully

Use digital platforms to support your community's goals:

- Explore productivity tools for group goal-setting and tracking
  - Use shared calendars for community events and challenges
  - Consider creating a community blog or newsletter

11. Encourage Leadership and Contribution

Empower members to take active roles in the community:

- Rotate responsibilities for organizing events or discussions
  - Encourage members to lead workshops on their areas of expertise
  - Create opportunities for members to mentor newcomers

12. Adapt and Evolve

Be open to changing your community's structure and focus as needed:

- Regularly seek feedback from members

- Be willing to try new formats or activities
- Stay flexible to accommodate the community's changing needs

13. Collaborate with Other Communities

Connect with other groups focused on digital wellness:

- Organize joint events or challenges
  - Share resources and best practices
  - Consider forming a larger network of digital minimalist communities

14. Maintain a Beginner's Mindset

Create a culture of continuous learning and growth:

- Encourage members to share new discoveries and insights
  - Be open to diverse perspectives on digital minimalism
  - Regularly revisit and refine community practices

15. Balance Online and Offline Community Building

While digital tools can facilitate community organization, prioritize offline connections:

- Encourage local subgroups for in-person activities
  - Plan annual or semi-annual retreats or conferences
  - Create opportunities for members to collaborate on real-world projects

Building a community of digital minimalists can provide invaluable support and motivation for those seeking to cultivate a healthier relationship with technology. By creating a space for shared learning, accountability, and connection, you can help others on their journey towards more intentional and balanced technology use.

Remember, the goal of teaching digital minimalism to others – whether children, friends and family, or a broader community – is not to enforce a rigid set of rules, but to inspire and support a more mindful approach to technology use. Each person's path to digital minimalism will be unique, influenced by their personal circumstances, goals, and challenges.

As you share these principles with others, remain open to learning from their experiences and insights as well. The landscape of digital technology is constantly evolving, and by fostering a community of individuals committed to intentional tech use, you create a powerful resource for navigating these changes together.

Ultimately, the spread of digital minimalism has the potential to create ripple effects far beyond individual lives. As more people adopt these practices, it can lead to broader societal shifts in how we design, use, and think about technology. By teaching digital minimalism to others, you're not just helping individuals – you're contributing to a larger movement towards a more balanced and human-centered digital world.

Staying Minimal in an Ever-Changing Digital Landscape

As we look to the future, it's clear that the digital landscape will continue to evolve at a rapid pace. New technologies, platforms, and digital challenges will emerge, potentially disrupting our carefully cultivated digital minimalist practices. This chapter explores strategies for adapting to these changes while maintaining a minimalist approach, predicting and preparing for future digital challenges, and examining the role digital minimalism might play in shaping technological development.

Adapting to New Technologies While Maintaining Minimalism

The key to staying minimal in the face of new technologies is to approach them with intention and mindfulness. Here are strategies for adapting to technological changes without compromising your digital minimalist principles:

1. Develop a Technology Evaluation Framework

Create a set of criteria for assessing new technologies:

- Does this technology align with my values and goals?
  - Will it significantly improve my life or work in a meaningful way?
  - Can I use it mindfully, or is it designed to be addictive?

- What are the potential downsides or risks?

2. Implement a Waiting Period

Resist the urge to adopt new technologies immediately:

- Establish a personal "waiting period" (e.g., 30 days) before adopting new tech
    - Use this time to research, observe others' experiences, and reflect on potential impacts

3. Start with Minimal Integration

When adopting new technology, begin with the most basic version or features:

- Gradually add features or increase usage only as needed
    - Regularly reassess if the technology is serving its intended purpose

4. Maintain Core Digital Minimalist Practices

As you incorporate new technologies, hold firm to foundational minimalist principles:

- Continue regular digital detoxes and tech-free times
    - Keep practicing mindful tech use, regardless of the platform
    - Regularly declutter your digital life, including new additions

5. Focus on Timeless Skills

Prioritize developing skills that transcend specific technologies:

- Critical thinking and information evaluation
    - Effective communication (both digital and in-person)
    - Time management and productivity

- Creativity and problem-solving

6. Stay Informed, Not Overwhelmed

Keep abreast of technological developments without getting caught up in every trend:

- Follow a few trusted sources for tech news
    - Engage in discussions about emerging technologies and their implications
    - Consider the broader impact of new technologies on society and individual well-being

7. Leverage New Technologies for Minimalism

Look for ways new technologies can support your minimalist goals:

- Explore AI and automation tools that can reduce digital busywork
    - Utilize advanced productivity features in new software to streamline workflows
    - Consider how emerging technologies (like augmented reality) might reduce the need for physical devices

8. Maintain a Questioning Mindset

Approach new technologies with a critical eye:

- Question the motives behind new platforms or features
    - Consider the long-term implications of adopting a new technology
    - Be willing to abandon technologies that don't align with your minimalist values

9. Adapt Minimalist Strategies to New Platforms

As new digital platforms emerge, develop minimalist usage strategies:

- Set clear boundaries and usage rules for each new platform
    - Look for built-in features that support mindful use
    - Be prepared to opt-out of platforms that don't allow for minimalist engagement

10. Embrace Selective Ignorance

Accept that you can't (and shouldn't) keep up with every new technology:

- Choose which areas of technological development to focus on based on your needs and interests
    - Practice being comfortable with not knowing about or using certain technologies

By applying these strategies, you can navigate the evolving digital landscape while maintaining your commitment to digital minimalism. Remember, the goal is not to resist all technological change, but to engage with new technologies in a way that enhances rather than detracts from your life.

Predicting and Preparing for Future Digital Challenges

While we can't know exactly what digital challenges the future will bring, we can make educated guesses based on current trends and prepare ourselves accordingly. Here are some potential future challenges and strategies for addressing them:

1. Increased AI Integration

Challenge: As AI becomes more prevalent in our daily lives, we may face new forms of digital overwhelm and privacy concerns.

Preparation:

- Educate yourself about AI capabilities and limitations
- Develop critical thinking skills to evaluate AI-generated content
- Establish clear boundaries for AI use in your personal and professional life
- Stay informed about AI privacy issues and take steps to protect your data

2. Virtual and Augmented Reality

Challenge: Immersive technologies may blur the lines between digital and physical experiences, potentially leading to increased escapism or digital addiction.

Preparation:

- Approach VR and AR with clear intentions and usage limits
- Prioritize real-world experiences and relationships
- Use immersive technologies as tools for specific purposes rather than default environments
- Be mindful of the physical and mental health impacts of prolonged use

3. Internet of Things (IoT) Expansion

Challenge: As more devices become "smart" and interconnected, we may face increased complexity in managing our digital lives.

Preparation:

- Carefully consider the necessity of smart features before purchasing new devices
- Regularly audit and declutter your IoT ecosystem
- Implement strong security practices for all connected devices
- Look for ways to simplify and streamline your IoT setup

4. Digital Health Monitoring

Challenge: The increase in digital health tracking may lead to obsessive self-monitoring and data anxiety.

Preparation:

- Set clear goals for health tracking and limit data collection to what's truly useful
- Practice periodic "data fasts" where you rely on bodily awareness rather than digital metrics
- Use health data as a tool for insight, not a source of stress or self-judgment
- Maintain a holistic view of health that includes non-quantifiable factors

5. Deepfakes and Misinformation

Challenge: Advanced AI-generated content may make it increasingly difficult to discern truth from fiction online.

Preparation:

- Develop strong media literacy skills
- Use multiple, reputable sources for important information
- Be cautious about sharing or acting on sensational content
- Support and advocate for technologies and policies that combat misinformation

6. Digital Inheritance

Challenge: As our digital lives become more complex, managing and passing on our digital assets may become a significant issue.

Preparation:

- Regularly declutter and organize your digital assets
- Create a digital estate plan, including instructions for handling your online accounts and data
- Consider the long-term implications of your digital footprint

- Use services that allow for legacy planning and account management

7. Brain-Computer Interfaces

Challenge: As brain-computer interfaces advance, we may face new questions about digital boundaries and cognitive privacy.

Preparation:
- Stay informed about the development and ethical implications of these technologies
- Carefully consider the privacy and security aspects before adopting such technologies
- Develop strong mental practices (like meditation) to maintain cognitive boundaries
- Advocate for strict ethical guidelines and regulations in this field

8. Digital Environmental Impact

Challenge: The environmental cost of our digital lives may become increasingly apparent and problematic.

Preparation:
- Be mindful of the environmental impact of your digital habits
- Opt for energy-efficient devices and practices
- Support companies and policies that prioritize sustainable technology
- Consider the necessity of upgrades and new purchases in light of environmental costs

9. Attention Economization

Challenge: As the attention economy grows, we may see new, more sophisticated attempts to capture and monetize our attention.

Preparation:
   - Strengthen your attention span through practices like meditation and deep work
   - Be vigilant about new platforms and features designed to hijack attention
   - Advocate for ethical design practices in technology
   - Cultivate hobbies and interests that don't rely on digital platforms

10. Digital Inequality

Challenge: As technology becomes more integral to daily life, the digital divide may widen, creating new forms of social and economic inequality.

Preparation:
   - Stay aware of digital inequality issues
   - Support initiatives that promote digital literacy and access
   - Consider the accessibility of your digital minimalist practices and be willing to adapt them for different contexts
   - Advocate for policies that address digital inequality

By anticipating these potential challenges, we can prepare ourselves to face the future digital landscape with resilience and intersectionality. Remember, the key is not to predict the future perfectly, but to develop adaptable mindsets and practices that can evolve with changing technology.

The Role of Digital Minimalism in Shaping Tech Development

As digital minimalism gains traction, it has the potential to influence the direction of technological development. Here's how digital minimalism might shape the future of tech:

1. Demand for Ethical Design

Digital minimalists may drive demand for technology designed with user well-being in mind:

- Increased interest in apps and platforms that promote focused work and reduced screen time
    - Pressure on tech companies to incorporate digital wellness features into their products
    - Growing market for devices and software that prioritize simplicity and intentional use

2. Shift in Metrics of Success

The rise of digital minimalism could change how tech companies measure success:

- Moving away from engagement metrics (time spent, clicks) towards value metrics (user satisfaction, goal achievement)
    - Increased emphasis on quality over quantity in user interactions
    - Growing importance of "time well spent" as a key performance indicator

3. Innovation in Minimalist Tech

We may see new technologies specifically designed to support digital minimalist lifestyles:

- Development of "calm technology" that integrates seamlessly into our lives without demanding attention
    - Creation of tools that help manage and reduce digital clutter
    - Innovation in interfaces that minimize cognitive load and maximize efficiency

4. Emphasis on Privacy and Control

Digital minimalism's focus on intentional use may drive advancements in user privacy and control:

- Development of more granular privacy settings and data control options
    - Increased transparency in how user data is collected and used
    - Innovation in decentralized and user-controlled technologies

5. Rethinking Notification Systems

The minimalist push against constant interruptions could lead to smarter, more considerate notification systems:

- AI-driven notifications that learn user preferences and only alert for truly important matters
    - Development of non-intrusive notification methods (e.g., ambient notifications)
    - Options for scheduled notification delivery to support focused work periods

6. Balancing Connectivity and Disconnection

Tech development may start to address the need for both connection and disconnection:

- Creation of "digital zones" in public spaces that support both tech use and tech-free experiences
    - Development of devices with easy-to-use disconnection features
    - Innovation in technologies that facilitate meaningful in-person connections

7. Sustainable Tech Practices

Digital minimalism's emphasis on intentional consumption may influence more sustainable tech practices:

- Development of longer-lasting, modular devices to reduce e-waste
    - Increased focus on energy-efficient technologies
    - Growth in refurbished and recycled tech markets

8. Redefinition of "Smart" Technology

The concept of "smart" devices may evolve to prioritize simplicity and user autonomy:

- Development of AI that enhances human decision-making rather than replacing it
    - Creation of IoT devices that offer genuine utility without unnecessary complexity
    - Focus on interoperability and open standards to reduce ecosystem lock-in

9. Evolution of Social Media

Digital minimalism could drive significant changes in social media platforms:

- Development of features that encourage meaningful interactions over passive scrolling
    - Creation of tools for users to better curate and control their social media experiences
    - Emergence of alternative social platforms designed around minimalist principles

10. Education and Digital Literacy

The spread of digital minimalism may influence educational technology and digital literacy efforts:

- Development of curricula that teach mindful technology use alongside traditional digital skills

- Creation of tools that help educators balance tech integration with offline learning experiences
- Increased emphasis on critical thinking and media literacy in tech education

11. Workplace Technology Evolution

Digital minimalism in professional settings could shape the development of workplace technologies:

- Creation of collaboration tools that respect focus time and reduce unnecessary interruptions
- Development of productivity software that encourages deep work and discourages multitasking
- Innovation in technologies that support healthy work-life boundaries in remote and hybrid work environments

12. Mindful AI Development

The principles of digital minimalism might influence the development of AI technologies:

- Focus on creating AI that augments human capabilities rather than replacing human involvement
- Development of AI systems with clear, understandable decision-making processes
- Creation of AI tools that help users make more intentional choices about their digital engagement

As digital minimalists become a more vocal and influential user group, their preferences and values may increasingly shape the direction of technological development. This influence has the potential to create a technological landscape that is more aligned with human well-being, intersectionality, and sustainable practices.

However, it's important to note that the impact of digital minimalism on tech development will depend on various factors, including market forces, regulatory environments, and broader societal trends. Digital minimalists can play a role in shaping this future by:

- Advocating for technologies that align with minimalist values
   - Supporting companies and initiatives that prioritize user well-being and ethical design
   - Participating in discussions and policy-making processes related to technology development
   - Sharing their experiences and insights to help others understand the benefits of a minimalist approach to technology

By actively engaging in these ways, practitioners of digital minimalism can contribute to a future where technology serves human needs and values more effectively, creating a digital landscape that enhances our lives without overwhelming them.

As we navigate this ever-changing digital future, the principles of digital minimalism – intersectionality, focus on value, and mindful engagement – will remain crucial guides. By staying true to these principles while remaining open to positive technological advancements, we can help shape a future where technology enriches our lives without dominating them.

Conclusion

As we reach the end of our journey through the principles and practices of digital minimalism, it's important to reflect on the transformative power of this approach to technology. Throughout this book, we've explored the challenges of our increasingly digital world and discovered strategies for creating a more intentional, balanced relationship with our devices and online spaces.

Recapping Our Digital Minimalism Journey

We began by recognizing the need for digital minimalism in our modern world, acknowledging the toll that information overload and constant connectivity can take on our mental clarity, productivity, and overall well-being. We then delved into the core principles of digital minimalism, understanding that it's not about rejecting technology outright, but about using it more purposefully and effectively.

Our exploration took us through practical strategies for decluttering our digital lives, from streamlining our devices and inboxes to curating our social media presence and digital content consumption. We learned the importance of creating sustainable digital routines, implementing regular digital detoxes, and fostering a mindful approach to technology use.

We also addressed the challenges of implementing digital minimalism in various aspects of our lives, including our professional environments and our relationships with friends and family. We discovered ways to advocate for digital wellness in our workplaces and communities, recognizing that our individual choices can have a ripple effect on those around us.

Finally, we looked to the future, considering how to maintain our digital minimalist practices in an ever-evolving technological landscape. We explored strategies for adapting to new technologies while staying true to our minimalist principles, and we considered the potential role of digital minimalism in shaping future tech development.

The Promise of a Clearer Digital Life

As we conclude, it's crucial to remember that digital minimalism is not about achieving perfection in our technology use. Rather, it's about cultivating a more intentional, balanced relationship with our digital tools. The promise of digital minimalism is a clearer, more focused life where technology serves our goals and values, rather than distracting from them.

By embracing digital minimalism, we can:

1. Reclaim our time and attention: By reducing digital clutter and setting clear boundaries, we free up mental space for what truly matters.

2. Enhance our productivity and creativity: With fewer digital distractions, we can engage in deeper, more focused work and creative pursuits.

3. Improve our relationships: By being more present in our interactions and less tethered to our devices, we can foster stronger, more meaningful connections.

4. Reduce stress and anxiety: Minimizing information overload and constant connectivity can lead to greater peace of mind and improved mental health.

5. Align our technology use with our values: Digital minimalism allows us to use technology in ways that support our goals and enhance our lives, rather than detract from them.

6. Increase our autonomy: By breaking free from addictive tech habits, we regain control over our choices and our time.

7. Foster deeper engagement with the world: With less time spent in the digital realm, we can more fully experience and appreciate the physical world around us.

Moving Forward: Your Digital Minimalism Journey

As you move forward from this book, remember that embracing digital minimalism is a personal journey. What works for one person may not work for another. The key is to find an approach that aligns with your unique needs, values, and circumstances.

Here are some final thoughts to guide you on your continued journey:

1. Start small: Begin with one or two strategies that resonate with you and gradually build from there.

2. Be patient with yourself: Changing ingrained digital habits takes time. Celebrate small victories and don't be discouraged by setbacks.

3. Stay flexible: As technology evolves and your life circumstances change, be willing to adjust your digital minimalist practices accordingly.

4. Reflect regularly: Take time to assess how your digital habits are impacting your life and whether they're aligned with your goals and values.

5. Share your experiences: By discussing your digital minimalism journey

with others, you can gain support, offer inspiration, and contribute to a broader conversation about healthy technology use.

6. Keep learning: Stay informed about new technologies and digital wellness strategies, always with an eye toward how they can support your minimalist goals.

7. Lead by example: Your mindful approach to technology can inspire others and contribute to a culture of more intentional digital use.

A Final Word

In our rapidly advancing digital age, the ability to use technology intentionally and effectively is becoming an increasingly valuable skill. By embracing digital minimalism, you're not just decluttering your digital life – you're cultivating a mindset and set of practices that will serve you well as technology continues to evolve.

Remember, the goal of digital minimalism is not to live a life devoid of technology, but to create a life where technology plays a supporting role in your pursuit of what you find meaningful and valuable. It's about using our remarkable digital tools to enhance our human experience, not to replace or diminish it.

As you continue on your digital minimalism journey, may you find greater clarity, focus, and fulfillment in both your digital and offline lives. Here's to a future where we are the masters of our technology, using it to build lives of purpose, connection, and joy.

Your journey towards a clearer, more intentional digital life starts now. Embrace it with optimism, patience, and the knowledge that each small step you take is leading you towards a more balanced, fulfilling relationship with technology. The digital world is vast and ever-changing, but with the principles of digital minimalism as your guide, you have the power to navigate it with intention, mindfulness, and grace.

www.ingramcontent.com/pod-product-compliance
Lightning Source LLC
LaVergne TN
LVHW051333050326
832903LV00031B/3514